Messiah

Hidden in the Ancient Feasts!

Dr. Sylvia Held

WestBow Press books may be ordered through booksellers or by contacting:

WestBow Press
A Division of Thomas Nelson & Zondervan
1663 Liberty Drive
Bloomington, IN 47403
www.westbowpress.com
1 (866) 928-1240

ISBN: 978-1-9736-0669-7 (sc)
ISBN: 978-1-9736-0670-3 (hc)
ISBN: 978-1-9736-0668-0 (e)

Library of Congress Control Number: 2017919453

Print information available on the last page.

WestBow Press rev. date: 06/12/2018

Matthew 11:28-30

11:28: “Come to Me, all who are weary and heavy-laden, and I will give you rest.

11:29: “Take My yoke upon you and learn from Me, for I am gentle and humble in heart, and YOU WILL FIND REST FOR YOUR SOULS.

11:30: “For My yoke is easy and My burden is light”.

Zondervan NASB Wide Margin Bible

Dedication

I want to dedicate this book first of all to my wonderful Savior, the Lord Jesus Christ, Messiah.

To my paternal grandmother, Estelle Narcissa Seligman, may she rest in the peace of Hashem.

To my wonderful husband, Harold A. Held, who has been my tireless supporter, encourager, and helper not only in this project but for the past thirty-six years of marriage.

Contents

Acknowlegement

I want to acknowledge two men of God whom I especially respect for their teaching, writing, and love of the Lord: Pastor Mark Biltz of El Shaddai Ministries and Messianic Rabbi Jonathan Cahn of Hope of the World. Without the knowledge they so generously share and their inspired teaching this book would never have been written.

I also want to acknowledge and thank my Graphic Artist, Greg Wasell of Kalispell, MT, for all his hard work in preparing my pencil drawn pictures for publication in this book.

Preface

When we walked into a Messianic Fellowship for the first time, my husband and I were greeted with "Shabbat Shalom" by an usher with a smile of welcome on his face. There was an immediate feeling of excitement and a sense of the Lord's presence. Later I learned that Shabbat Shalom is a traditional Hebrew greeting used to wish one Sabbath peace. Having grown up in a non-religious family, the Sabbath wasn't kept as special. While I always sensed that there was a God in heaven who looked over us, I wasn't introduced to Yeshua Jesus as my personal Savior as a child. Even so, I loved to attend Sunday School and at the age of five I walked the four blocks from my house to a neighborhood church each Sunday and whenever allowed, would stay for church services. There was something comforting about the sanctuary with its large picture of Jesus on the wall behind the altar that drew me in. The church wasn't fancy. It was a simple wooden, country church common in the southern part of the United States. The start of the service was announced with a man pulling on a rope, by the double front doors, which rang the large bell in the bell tower on the roof. The church had tall glass windows on each side of the sanctuary and wooden pews and wooden floors. It smelled like old wood. I remember trying to figure out how to sing the songs in the hymn book. I was too young to understand that with each line you sang, you had to skip a line or two to complete the verse. People sure could pray in that old wooden church! And in the summer, they periodically had picnics out on the front lawn. The food was all home-made and tasted delicious!

I will never forget the day when I felt the presence of the Holy Spirit for the first time. I was about twelve years old. I was sitting in the sanctuary at the end of the service when all of the sudden the pastor asked people to come forward if they wanted to join the church. I immediately felt warm and excited. I didn't know exactly what it was at the time, but I knew it was from God. I thought if I joined the church I would feel even closer to God. I didn't realize, nor was I told, that salvation is by grace through faith in Jesus alone. What I did understand was that I had to get my mother's permission to join the church or she would be angry, so I ran home to ask her if I could join the church. I will never forget her response. She said, "no daughter of mine is going to join that church"! She pulled me out of that small church I loved and the next Sunday sent me to a large, red brick church of her choice downtown. It felt so cold with its white walls, white pews and red carpet. That day, in that church, I lost my contact with God. I felt so sad and lost. I know now that He was there all the time but at that time He seemed so far away. Through the years I sought Him through prayer from time to time but I felt like He never heard me. I gave up and went the way of the world, empty, without God to comfort and direct me. It took me until I was thirty-five years old to find God again and to celebrate His Sabbath with other born-again believers.

At the age of thirty-five I was suffering emotionally. My marriage of fifteen years was over and I felt so uncertain about what the future held in store; how I would go on. My sons had both decided to stay with their father who had said he could provide for their needs financially better than I could, and I was alone. One evening I turned on the television and happened to hear Oral Roberts speaking. I was instantly mesmerized. Those in attendance appeared to have a glow on their faces. By the end of the service I prayed the sinner's prayer. I immediately felt the joy of the Lord return. That was on a Thursday night. I couldn't wait to go to church on Sunday!! Within five months I was blessed with the baptism of the Holy Spirit and I began to understand the Bible in an entirely new way. I began to realize how awesome God is; that He has more wonderful plans for my life than I could ever imagine. He is more majestic, loving, and amazing and His love is deeper than the depths of the sea! He healed my wounds and blessed me with a husband who loved both me and God completely. It is sad to think what I would have missed had God not intervened in my life. He picked me up, dusted me off, and gave me His unconditional love, and the blessing of the baptism of the Holy Spirit.

For thirty-six years my husband and I had primarily attended non-denominational churches. It was when I began hearing the same sermons over and over again that I started asking the Lord to direct me to a place where I could learn more about Him and His Word. After a year of prayer He led me to El Shaddai Ministries on-line. I was thrilled!! Soon afterwards, my husband and I both started listening to El Shaddai Ministries with Pastor Mark Biltz every Saturday morning. Several times a year we drove 9 hours to attend services at his church. He introduced us to the importance of understanding the Jewish roots of our Christian faith. We learned how Yeshua, Hebrew for Jesus, had fulfilled the Spring Feasts as outlined in Leviticus 23 at His first coming, and the fact that He will fulfill the Fall Feasts at His Second Coming. I was hooked! I wanted to learn all I could about the feasts of the Lord, so I began to research and read everything I could find! As I shared with others the things I was learning, they got excited and asked me to either teach a class on the Feasts or write a book about them. The result of their enthusiasm, my husband's encouragement, and the Holy Spirit nudging me, I wrote this book. It is my sincere desire that God will be glorified through my efforts and that other Christians will come to understand the importance of studying our Jewish roots.

Note: the Hebrew name for our Messiah is Yeshua which means "salvation". The name Yeshua was translated into Greek as Iesus and was later written as Jesus.

Introduction

Over and over again people have asked me why I was interested in studying the Feasts of the Lord. Some people believe that as Christians, we no longer need to study the Old Testament because they say the New Testament has replaced it. Such statements show a lack of knowledge about the fact that God's plan for our salvation through Yeshua Jesus is hidden in the ancient feasts. If we don't understand the feasts and God's appointed times as "dress rehearsals" of what is to come in the future, we truly can't understand the New Testament and what Yeshua Jesus was telling us. As I prayed about what I could do, I felt the Lord's Holy Spirit nudge me to write a book on why it is important for Christians study all of the Lord's feasts and understand God's plan for the Gentiles who are grafted into His kingdom as part of His Jewish family.

Disclaimer: In my preparation for writing this book, I decided to use the New American Standard Bible by Zondervan and The Complete Jewish Study Bible by Hendrickson as the sources for my biblical quotes. All quotes are from the NASB unless otherwise noted.

13 Reasons Why Christians Should Celebrate the Feasts of the Lord

1. The Scriptures tell anyone who reads Leviticus 23 that the feasts are the Feasts of the Lord, not feasts for the Jewish people only. These appointed times by the Lord are to be celebrated by all of God's children, whether Jew or Gentile.

2. The Scripture shows us in the New Testament that Messiah Yeshua celebrated the feasts when He was on the earth and if He did, so should we.
3. The most important dates when we are to celebrate God's feasts days are in the Old Testament. They tell us when and where we are to meet with Him and are dress rehearsals for how the feasts connect with our faith in the Messiah.
4. We can't possibly understand prophecy without first understanding the meaning of the feasts and their appointed times on the Hebrew calendar.
5. Messiah died on Passover, was in the grave on Unleavened Bread, and rose on First
   Fruits during His First Coming during the Spring feasts. If He fulfilled the Spring Feasts on the dates pre-ordained, doesn't it stand to reason that He will fulfill the Fall Feasts to come on their pre-set dates?
6. In Leviticus 23 we are told the Feasts are to be kept as a perpetual statute throughout all generations; and since God is the same yesterday, today, and forever, we believers need to obey His instructions and keep the Feasts.
7. Through understanding the meaning of the Feasts in depth, we can develop a deeper understanding of our Savior, Yeshua Jesus, who is celebrated in the Feasts.
8. It is so important to God that He preplanned the day His Son, Our Savior, would die.
   It was not a second thought or a Plan B. God the Father had David write the Psalms that would be sung at Messiah's death 1000 years before He died.
9. The Passover, for example, helps us understand the stages of our salvation – our sanctification, deliverance, redemption, and our acceptance into the Kingdom of God – Pastor Mark Biltz.
10. By understanding the meaning of the feasts, and their appointed times on the Hebrew calendar, we can glean an understanding of the future events and when they will occur as related to Yeshua Jesus; the Rapture, the Millennial Reign, the Marriage Supper of the Lamb, the New Jerusalem, and the Sabbath rest in heaven.

11. Yeshua Jesus established the memorial of Communion during the Passover Seder. Both Passover and Communion represents the fellowship between God and man. They are meant to be observed as a memorial forever. They are like eating at God's own table.
12. By understanding the Feasts of the Lord we better understand not only our Messiah but also our Christian faith and its Jewish roots.
13. By understanding the Feasts we can better understand our wonderful Salvation and Atonement.

SHABBAT SHALOM

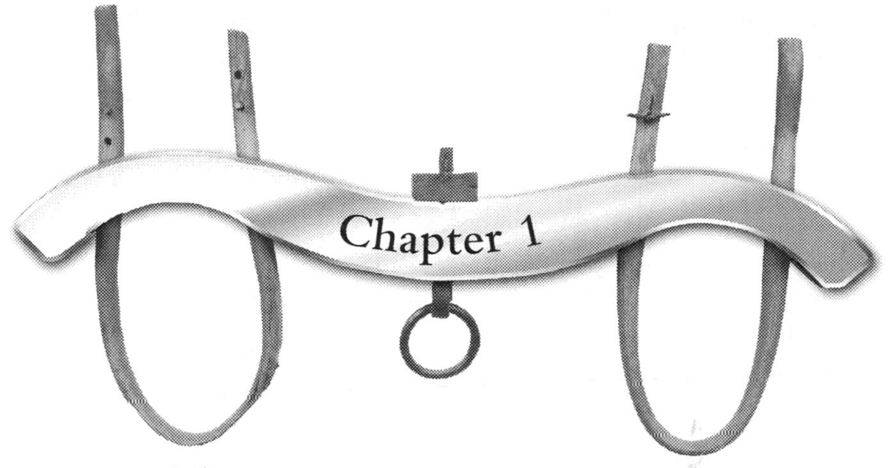

Chapter 1

The Feast of the Lord's Sabbath

Leviticus 23:1-3 says: "The Lord spoke again to Moses, saying, "Speak to the sons of Israel, and say to them, 'The Lord's appointed times [*mo'ed*] which you shall proclaim as holy convocation - My appointed times are these: For six days work may be done; but on the seventh day there is a Sabbath of complete rest, a holy convocation. You shall not do any work; it is a Sabbath to the Lord in all your dwellings.'"

The Sabbath commemorates God's creation of the heavens, the earth and all He made. It was the first divinely appointed feast by the Lord and is therefore essential for all believers to honor it. God spoke of the importance of the Sabbath more often than any other feast in the Torah. Tom Stapleton pointed out when one looks at the word S-**a-b-b-a** t h the thing one notices immediately is the name of God, ABBA which means "daddy", is in the central letters that make up the word. He further pointed out that "the Sabbath is the cornerstone feast" and all other feasts follow it. Genesis 2:3 says, "Then God blessed the seventh day and sanctified it, because on it He rested from all His work which God had created and made". Man is to rest on the Sabbath just as God rested on the seventh day. God wants His children to set aside the Sabbath and to joyfully look forward to it throughout the week. Many ancient books speak of the benefits of spending time with God on the Sabbath. We are reminded that when on individual takes time to stop their daily activities, they are free to study the Word of God which renews their mind, and allows them to gain understanding of the things of the spirit. It is a time to worship the Lord and to thank Him for all the blessings He has given to us.

The Sabbath was given before the fall of Adam and Eve and their expulsion by God from the Garden of Eden. The need to remove them must have broken the heart of the Father. But in His love, He knew it had to be done; for if they were not removed, and they ate of the forbidden fruit again, they would live eternally in an unredeemed state.

How God must have looked forward to walking with Adam and Eve in the cool of the day in the garden He had made for them. Even after their fall, when the heart of the Father was broken, He still reached out in love to the children He created and personally made them clothing of animal skins even though He knew they had disobeyed Him and had sinned. This was the first animal sacrifice mentioned in the Scriptures. How awful it must have been for Adam and Eve to realize they had been deceived by the serpent in the garden, were naked, ashamed, and were no longer covered in the Shekinah light of God! Adam had no excuse. God had personally told him not to eat from the tree of the knowledge of good and evil. Adam had communicated that to Eve. Still he chose to disobey and sin.

In our world today, many people refuse to honor the Sabbath and many others disagree on which day the Sabbath day should be kept. The Muslims worship Allah on the sixth day of the week, the Jews worship God on the seventh day like they were commanded to do on Mount Sinai, and most Christian denominations worship on the first day of the week, in remembrance of the day Yeshua Jesus rose from the dead. "Both Islam and Christianity openly admit that their Sabbath is not the biblical Sabbath", wrote Boaz Michael from The Fruits of Zion. The book of Genesis tells us that God chose the seventh day after Creation as His day of rest, and Yeshua Jesus never changed it to another day. God knew that man needed a day to rest, a fact that has been proven through research studies in science and biology, so He set the pattern for man to follow. God also wants His children to fellowship with Him because He loves us and He wants to bless us. The Sabbath is so important to God that it was included as part of the Ten Words [Commandments] He gave to Moses on Mount Sinai.

The Sabbath Meal

In Israel the day begins on sundown on Friday and ends at sundown on Saturday; from 6:00 pm on one evening to 6:00 pm the next evening. Their day follows the pattern set forth by God in Genesis 1:2-4. It says, ... and darkness was over the surface of the deep... and God said, let there be light...and God saw that the light was good and God separated the light from the darkness. The Sabbath meal therefore is held at sundown on Friday. It is meant to be a very joyful, holy, and God honoring experience. Isaiah 58:13-14 speaks of keeping the Sabbath. The Lord asks that we to cease work and not to engage in our own pleasurable things on His holy day. Isaiah 58:13 says, "And call the Sabbath a delight, the holy day of the Lord honorable". If one adheres to this command, then that person will "ride on the heights of the earth"- Isaiah 58:14.

The brief summary presented here in this book fails to do justice to the beauty and blessings received by doing a Friday night Shabbat supper. Complete directions on how to conduct an evening Shabbat meal have been written by Susie McElroy in her book: Erev Shabbat: A Believer Guide to the Evening Sabbath Meal. This writer is presenting a brief summary from Susie McElroy's work.

First, the wife or mother of the house puts a white tablecloth and white napkins on the table. Two white candles are placed in the center of the table. Two loaves of fresh challah bread, covered with a white cloth, are also placed on the table along with a bottle of grape juice or wine. A small bowl of saltwater is placed on the table so the bread can be dipped in it. A bowl of water and a hand towel are placed near the father's place at the head of the table so he can wash and dry his hands. Additional candles or tea lights are placed on the table for each woman who will be joining the family for dinner. A shofar is blown to welcome in the Sabbath. The woman of the house, with head covered, begins the meal with a blessing to usher in the Sabbath and lights the two center candles. At the same time, any female guests who are present light their tea lights. All the women recite the blessing which says, "Blessed are

You, Lord our God, King of the universe, who sanctifies us with His commandments and commanded us to be a light to the nations and who gave to us Yeshua our Messiah, the Light of the world. Amen". Husbands face their wives and bless them by quietly saying the blessing from Psalm 31 over her. Single men can say the blessing as a reminder that they too are part of the bride of Messiah. Wives face their husbands and bless their husbands by quieting repeating Psalm 1 over them. A blessing for the son(s) is based on Genesis 48:20. A blessing for the daughter(s) is based on Ruth 4:11. The leader then prays the Aaronic blessing over all the guests at the table. This blessing is found in Numbers 6:24-26. A prayer for Israel is given which is based on Deuteronomy 30:4-5 and said every Sabbath in every synagogue around the world. The Kiddush/ blessing over the wine is said together by all present. Wine is a symbol of joy in Psalm 104:15 as is the Sabbath. Everyone lifts up their wine glass and say this blessing together: "Blessed are You, Lord our God, King of the Universe, Creator of the fruit of the vine. Amen". Then a toast is given for the health of all present. It ends with the Hebrew saying, "L'Chaim" which means, "to life". The father or leader takes the bowl of water around to each member, beginning with his wife. They dip their right hand and then their left hand into the bowl and dry them on the towel provided as he says, "We wash our hands as a visual reminder that Yeshua has washed us clean by His blood and given us the Living Waters of the Holy Spirit". Wash hands now. Another blessing is said from Psalm 24:3-4. Next is the blessing over the bread. The challah bread is passed around the table and everyone takes a small piece. It is then dipped in salt and everyone eats the bread together. "Salt represents an everlasting covenant before the Lord" – Numbers 18:19. It is now time to enjoy your Sabbath meal! Afterwards everyone says a blessing from Deuteronomy 8:10.

The Sabbath meal is meant to be a time when the entire family gathers together to eat, to fellowship, and spend quality time with each other, and connect with each other's lives. It is a time when the family unit gives thanks to God for the many blessings He has given each of them during the week, and to sing songs of praise to Him, for as the Scripture says, "great is the Lord, and [He is] greatly to be praised"- Psalm 48:1. It is meant to be a dress rehearsal for things to come in the future kingdom age when Messiah reigns. If we follow the pattern as God instructed there would be fewer problems in marriages, in families, and in the world. Unfortunately in today's modern world, parents don't often know what their children think about, how they feel about things or what is happening in their daily lives. Everyone stays hidden behind the screen of their electronic devices or come home exhausted after working long hours away from home rather than making time with family a priority. This behavior creates feelings of alienation and loneliness that lead to depression, emptiness, addictions, suicides, homicides, and other forms of acting out behavior.

A Story of a Sabbath Gathering

It was almost sundown and time for the Sabbath to begin. All week Moriah had counted off the days leading to the Sabbath. Everything she did was focused on it. Everything about it was a reminder of the importance of this day to G-d, and her relationship with Him. She thought about how G-d said in Exodus 20:8 to remember the Sabbath and keep it holy; and how Isaiah called the Sabbath a day of rest and a delight. She believed if she obeyed His commands, she would ride on the heights of the earth, because G-d said so.

Her heart pounded in anticipation at the thought of flying over the landscape of Jerusalem with G-d as her guide!

The table has been set with a special white Sabbath cloth. A small bowl of salt water representing the everlasting covenant of the Lord was set near where her father would sit as head of the table. Moriah eagerly watched as her Mother set the two fresh loaves of challah bread they had baked that afternoon on the table. As soon as everyone was seated, her Mother lit the candles and the room became alight with their glow. Moriah especially loved it when the shofar was blown to welcome in the Sabbath. It was like hearing the voice of G-d. Then, all the ladies present, got to join together in the prayer for the Sabbath blessing. It was wonderful! Her dad then pours a small glass of wine or grape juice for himself and for each family member and any guest who was present. His face was aglow as he prayed the Kiddush over the wine, "Blessed are You, Lord our God, King of the Universe, Creator of the fruit of the vine. Amen". Once the meal was blessed, her father would share verses from the Torah. Then as the family and friends were eating their meal, conversation and laughter filled the room. After all she thought, the Sabbath was meant to be a happy, G-d honoring time; a day to thank G-d for the blessings He had given to each of them. As the meal ended, an additional blessing of thankfulness was said and Moriah wondered if it would be like this in heaven. She once had heard her family talk excitedly about a wedding that was to take place among their friends. She remembered hearing them say that a wedding is like the Sabbath. So that must be how heaven is; a day to rest, to enjoy conversations, and a time to focus only on G-d. The Sabbath meal ended all too soon with everyone toasting to the health of all present and repeating the ancient Hebrew words, "L'Chaim" – to life!

How the Sabbath is Like a Wedding

To the Jewish people the Sabbath is like a wedding and should be considered by all as beautiful and royal just like a bride. It should be looked forward to with anticipation just like a bride joyfully anticipates her wedding and is clothed in her most beautiful raiment. When we turn off the noise and distractions of modern life, we can experience the Sabbath as God intended and experience a renewal of His spirit that the Father has placed within us. We can commune with God, our Creator and experience His Shalom. When the Sabbath is observed as God ordained it, it becomes a dress rehearsal for the Sabbath rest believers will experience in heaven. It is also a picture of a bridegroom who was freed from work on the day of his wedding so he can think only about his beautiful bride and the love he feels for her. This is how God thinks of His creation and this is why the Sages compared the Sabbath to a bride.

To the Jews: the Sabbath is like a wedding ring given by G-d, the Groom, to Israel His bride.

To the Christians: the Sabbath is a day in which one sings praises to God in thankfulness for all of His blessings, worships Him in spirit and truth, and learns about His Word and His will for our lives. It is a day to rest from our labors.

There are many places in the Scripture that refer to Israel as the bride and to God as the bridegroom. Isaiah says: "For as a young man marries a virgin, so your sons will marry you; and as the bridegroom rejoices over the bride, so your God will rejoice over you. God delights in her, and your land, married, for the Lord delights in you, and to Him your land will be married". These verses show us how special and meaningful the Sabbath is to God. Without it mankind has no soul. It is a sign of the covenant entered into by God and His creation for all generations. The Scripture tells us in Genesis 2:3 that God blessed and sanctified the seventh day, and so must man sanctify the seventh day. Father God wants it to be as meaningful to man as it is meaningful to Him. God-honoring Jews believe that six days without a Sabbath is like a bridegroom who works hard to create a beautiful bridal chamber but has no bride to enjoy it with.

The Sabbath reminds us of our holy, covenant relationship with God. It sets us apart to Him alone, just as the bride is set apart for her bridegroom. It is time for His redeemed to serve His purposes and for His glory. It is a type of the Messianic Age in heaven in which we will enjoy true Sabbath peace for eternity. It is the day we look toward to with anticipation and joy.

The Sabbath Service

Eight Psalms are recited by the Jewish people on the Sabbath. But first the Sabbath has to be received and connected with by the people who are present. As believers we must embrace the Sabbath before the Lord's Sabbath can come. After the Psalms are read the La'cha dodi, translated as "come my beloved" is read. In this reading the rabbi speaks of the Sabbath as a bride. In the La'cha dodi God calls Israel His delight and says that the land will no longer be called "desolate". Then Isaiah 11:1 is read which refers to the Messiah. It says: "Then a shoot will spring from the stem of Jesse, and a branch from his roots will bear fruit". Christian believers know that Yeshua Jesus is the Messiah, who is called the Branch, and who is from the stem of Jesse. As we read on in Isaiah 11:2-5 it further describes Yeshua and His role. It says: "The Spirit of the Lord will rest on Him, the spirit of wisdom and understanding, the spirit of counsel and strength, the spirit of knowledge and the fear of the Lord. And He will delight in the fear of the Lord, and He will not judge by what His eyes see, Nor make a decision by what His ears hear; But with righteousness He will judge the poor, and decide with fairness for the afflicted of the earth; and He will strike the earth with the rod of His mouth, and with the breath of His lips He will slay the wicked. Also righteousness will be the belt about His lions, and faithfulness the belt about His waist".

The Sabbath service ends with the reading of the Shema, a foundational prayer for both Jewish and Messianic believers. It reads: "Hear O Israel, the Lord Our God, The Lord is One, Praise be the name of His glorious Sovereignty, Forever and Ever. Amen"! Then the service ends with asking the Lord to allow each person to rest in peace and experience life through the resurrection as He spreads His wings, like a canopy, over us in His tabernacle.

The Shema is so important to Judaism and Messianic Christians that children are taught it at a very young age. They are told to cover their eyes when they hear the name Adonai as a way to honor the God of Israel. This inadvertently became a very important form of identification for Jewish children after World War II.

One day a Jewish rabbi went to a Catholic orphanage in search of Jewish children that had been hidden there from the Nazis and the Holocaust. As he inquired about the children he was told there were no Jewish children there, only Christians. He decided to say the Shema to see if he was being told the truth. As he said the Shema, the Jewish children covered their eyes as they had been taught prior to the war. By this action, the rabbi was able to identify the Jewish children, take them out of the orphanage, and return them to their remaining family members.

A Personal Story

I remember a few years ago when my husband and I were in Jerusalem. We had been on a tour all day and were tired and hungry by the time we arrived back to our hotel. Upon arrival, we noticed a group of Jewish families all dressed up in their finest apparel. The ladies and little girls were dressed in black satin dresses, and the men in black suits with white shirts, and black hats of various styles, with some trimmed in velvet. They were waiting to attend a Sabbath service in the hotel. I, for one, immediately felt convicted! I was aware of my dusty blue jeans and disheveled appearance. When our group was finally called into the dining room and taken to our tables, our leader led us in a prayer of thanksgiving for our meal and for the wonderful experiences we had during our journey. Once we stopped for a moment, connected with the Lord in prayer, both honored and acknowledged Him, we felt His presence with us like a sweet welcoming breeze on a warm summer day. The more we acknowledged Yeshua as our Lord and Savior, the more His presence was felt, and His blessings began to fill our hearts. God is faithful and longs to be with His children. He loves to love and bless them as a good parent loves to give gifts to their children. This felt like a Sabbath and the Lord gave us rest.

The Counsel of Nicea and the Sabbath

The first ecumenical council of the Christian Church was held in the city of Nicea in Constantinople around 325 AD. The purpose of the meeting was to address several major issues that were about to split the church. The bishops were concerned about the following six issues: prejudice, paganism and anti-Semitism that had invaded the church, the arguments concerning the meaning of the writings of the apostles on the nature of God and Jesus, and the days on which to celebrate Easter and the Sabbath. At the same time, Constantine was trying to unite the kingdom under his headship. Being the consummate politician, he knew if the differences remained unresolved in the church they could end up destroying his chances of ruling over a united kingdom. To keep that from happening, he ordered the bishops of the church to appear before him in Nicea. He wanted to join with them in resolving the disagreements and by so doing solve the controversy that was dividing the church and the kingdom. To ensure the bishops attendance, Constantine generously paid their way to the meeting. Once they arrived, he treated them with honor. By so doing they agreed to allow him to attend their meeting, over which he eventually presided. "It was decided that God and Jesus were 'of one substance'; and that 'the Son had absolute equality with the Father'" – Encyclopedia Britannica.

The bishops worked diligently to settle on one specific day to celebrate Easter. Because of the growth of anti-Semitism, the bishops wanted that day to be different from the day the Jews were celebrating Passover. The problem they encountered, however, was the fact that Easter and Passover had historically occurred on the same day. Try as they might, they could not solve the problem satisfactorily. In an attempt to solve the problem they kept changing the date for Easter on the calendar. It got to the point where the Christian church was celebrating the resurrection of the Lord as much as a month before Yeshua Jesus actually died!

The next point of contention was which day should be recognized as the Sabbath. The Bishop of Rome insisted that the Christian Sabbath day should be on Sunday. This was his way of separating the church from Judaism; a separation that has not served either the church or the Jewish community well.

Satan works to divide, conquer, and destroy God's people any way he can, and one of his favorite tools is anti-Semitism; but he can't outsmart our God. The Jews are God's chosen people, and the Gentile is grafted in as spiritual Jews. We are one body, and more and more Christians are studying the Jewish roots of their Christian faith. The Scriptures tell us in Genesis 2:3 that the Sabbath was blessed and sanctified by God on the seventh day of Creation. It is therefore often held on Saturday in many places around the world. While the Sabbath day was never officially changed to Sunday, it remains to be kept on both days. As Sam Hadler pointed out, "the real issue is not the day, but are you redeemed by, relating to, and resting in the Lord"? It bears noting, that while anti-Semitism remains a major problem in the churches that teach Replacement Theology and other false doctrines, one major positive outcome of the Counsel of Nicea was the Nicene Creed which clarified the basic beliefs of the Christian faith.

Today, the Jews, Messianic believers, and some Christian denominations keep Saturday as the Sabbath although most of the Christian churches keep Sunday as the Sabbath. In reality, God wants us to acknowledge and fellowship with Him everyday. He desires His children to be united in their acceptance of Yeshua Jesus as their Savior.

Thus the main question is, have you been saved from the curse of sin through your faith, and acceptance of Yeshua Jesus as Lord and Savior, and if not, why not? Why do you struggle against God instead of resting in Yeshua's provision for you? Is one day spent with God out of seven days to much to ask? The day chosen for the Sabbath is not as important as the quality of your relationship with the Creator and the importance placed on Him. His role needs to be meaningful and give significance in a person's life. The outcome of not honoring the Sabbath as the Lord intended would be emptiness rather than happiness and holiness in one's life. There is more to the Sabbath, however, than just honoring it. We must connect deeply with the spirit of it and partake of everything it has to offer to us. It is a reflection of God Himself and His loving care for us. As we surrender our lives to God's care, we become a recipient of His joy and blessings. Even when life turns out differently than we thought, and we feel hopeless or sad, we can trust that God is working all things together for those who love Him and are called according to His purposes. He is faithfully teaching the lessons He wants His children to learn. In order to learn what He wants us to know, it is important that we take time out of our busy schedules and lives to reflect with awe those sacred moments God has given to us; when He has communed with us and when He gave us insights into a Scripture, a person or a situation. Becoming aware of these moments draws us closer to Him and creates in us a desire to praise and thank Him for all He has done in our lives. This is why we need to follow His Sabbath as He ordained it. It is meant to be a time set apart to draw us closer not only to our fellow man, but especially to God who created all things. He created human beings as a spirit and soul encased in a body of dust. As such, we and we alone are the only created beings in the Universe that are able to procreate another soul. While we live, God blesses us. He gives us His love and the Holy Spirit to guide us in His Word and in our lives. When a redeemed person dies their soul and spirit returns to the Lord and He will dwell with them and they dwell with Him throughout eternity. The cycle of life is now complete. Thus it was on the seventh day of Creation when God created the Sabbath that the world was completed and with it mankind gained a corresponding sense of eternity. It was meant to be a foreshadow of the millennial reign of Yeshua Jesus, the Messiah, the King of Kings, and Lord of Lords -Revelation 19:16, but has been corrupted by Satan who has roamed on the earth since the fall of man seeking someone to devour.

In Exodus 20:8 God said: "Remember the Sabbath day, to keep it holy". While the Sabbath was intended by God to be a day of rest from our labors and treated as holy and beautiful, in our modern age of hustle and bustle, the quietness and holiness of the Sabbath is often lost in the midst of noise, busyness, and demands. Time with God is all too often substituted with worldly activities. Many people say, there just aren't not enough hours in a day to get everything completed. But in the mindset of the devout Jew, the Sabbath is the day when the heaven is opened and they get a glimpse of the God's plan and a sense of the world to come. It is meant to be rest from all the things in the world that are distracting us. We need to remember God created the Sabbath for man, not man for the Sabbath.

How Yeshua Fulfilled the Sabbath

The Hebrew day starts at sundown and ends on the following sundown, therefore Yeshua' last day on earth is considered by many researchers to have started at sundown on Thursday. Yeshua accomplished His entire task of redemption in one day by being crucified on the cross/pole. This act of love took place on Nisan 14th, the day of Passover. He was the Passover Lamb, sacrificed for our redemption. Now we who believe in Him can release everything to Him because of the cross. As we release all our sins, He is faithful and just to forgive them and places them "as far as the east is from the west". As a result, we experience rest for our souls.

Yeshua Jesus always puts human needs above ceremonial observances of the Sabbath. His actions, however, weren't always understood by the priests. They often became angry at Him for healing people on the Sabbath. They considered His actions a form of work which they prohibited. This was, however, one of the ways Yeshua Jesus fulfilled the intent of the Sabbath.

Yeshua Jesus came at the exact time that the Prophet Daniel predicted and was cut off as Daniel said. He will return a second time and fulfill the Fall Feasts on schedule. The time between His two comings is known as the age of the church. After the church is removed through the Rapture, God will again focus on Israel. Until the Rapture, it is up to all born-again believers to draw as many of the Jewish people as possible to their Messiah. We must introduce the Jews to Messiah by restoring His character that has been demeaned for 2,000 years. Messiah Yeshua has said He will not return until the Jewish people cry out, "blessed is He who comes in the name of the Lord"- Mark 11:9. Many pastors have suggested that this cry by Jewish believers in Yeshua Jesus as their Messiah won't occur until the end of the Tribulation Period.

Celebration of the Feasts

Unleaved Bread = Tomb

Passover = Cross

First Fruits = Resurrection

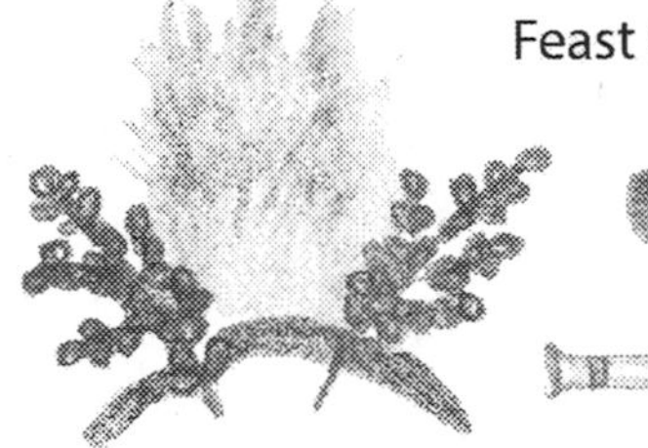

Feast Of Trumpets

Yom Kippur =
Book Of Life

Feast Of Pentecost

Feast Of Chanukah
(Hanukkah)

Feast Of Tabernacles

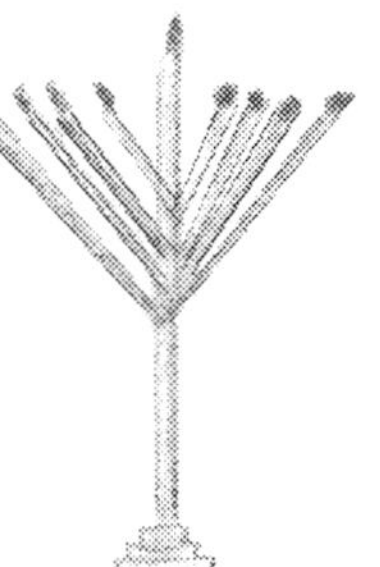

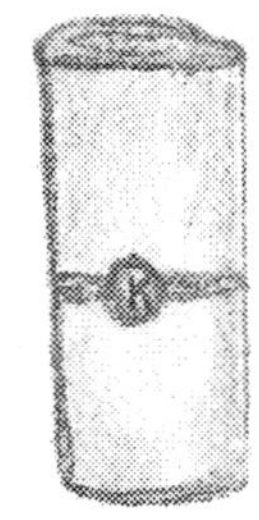

Feast of Purim

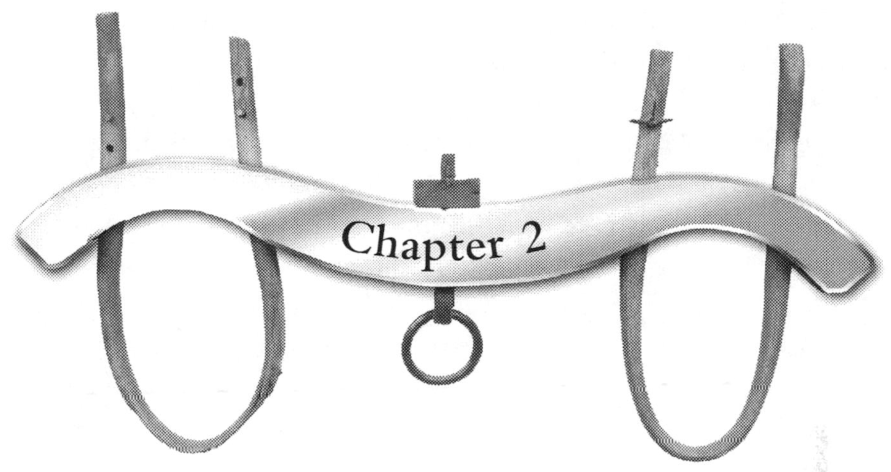

An Overview of the Seven Feasts of the Lord and Their Appointed Times; Pentecost, and Two National Celebrations

The order of the Feasts of the Lord as given from God to Moses begins with the Spring feasts: Passover, Feast of Unleavened Bread, and the Feast of First Fruits. These feasts mark the beginning of the harvest year which starts on Nisan 1. Shavuot known as Pentecost, occurs in mid-Summer. The Fall feasts are: Rosh Hashanah/Feast of Trumpets, Yom Kippur/Day of Atonement, and Feast of Tabernacles/Sukkot. These feasts occur at the end of the harvest season. Two additional national celebrations are kept yearly by the Jewish people: Purim which is held in Spring, just prior to Passover and Hanukkah which is held in the Winter.

The seven feasts of the Lord as commanded to Moses are found in order in Leviticus 23. It begins with the Lord instructing Moses what to say to the sons of Israel concerning the feasts He proclaimed.

Leviticus 23:2-4 says: "Speak to the sons of Israel and say to them, 'the Lord's appointed times which you shall proclaim as holy convocations – My appointed times are these: 'For six days work may be done, but on the seventh day there is a Sabbath of complete rest, a holy convocation. You shall not do any work; it is a Sabbath to the Lord in all your dwellings.

These are the appointed times of the Lord, holy convocations which you shall proclaim at the times appointed for them".

Almost 3,000 years ago the prophet Isaiah declared that God's people were to "Prepare the way of the Lord". To help His people prepare for the time of Yeshua Jesus' visitation, Father God set forth appointed times during the year on which to meet with Him. These appointed times were called the Feasts of the Lord and were actually meant to be an invitation to and a dress rehearsal for the Lord Messiah's First Coming. The redeemed can celebrate the Feasts now as we await His Second Coming. According to Jonathan Bernis, "one's acceptance of the invitation to participate in these feasts is not done out of a feeling of obligation, but done out of a desire to honor God and obey His instruction".

The Spring feasts were fulfilled during Yeshua Jesus' First Coming. The Fall Feasts have yet to be fulfilled by Yeshua Jesus, but will be fulfilled on the very day and hour at the time scheduled for His Second Coming. The feast between the Spring and Fall Feasts is most commonly called "the Feast of Weeks" or "Shavuot" by the Jews and "Pentecost" by believers in Yeshua Jesus.

To the Jews: it is a feast that commemorates the giving of the Torah by God to Moses.

To the Christians: Pentecost honors the day the church of Messiah was supernaturally born in Jerusalem and honors the outpouring of the Holy Spirit upon His disciples.

Yeshua Jesus gave the Holy Spirit as His betrothal gift to His bride. The betrothal gift was given to the bride as a promise that He will return someday and take His bride to His Father's house in heaven. There the bride of Yeshua will be with Him for eternity. Thus the Spring Feasts give us a picture of Yeshua Jesus' life, suffering, burial, and resurrection. The Fall feasts give believers a beautiful picture of the bridegroom coming back to earth with His church; those believers who were Raptured prior to the Tribulation Period. They will join with Messiah as He gathers the remnant of His bride to Himself that were left on the earth. This remnant consists of those Jews who recognized Him as their Messiah during the Tribulation Period.

A Closer Look at the Three Spring Feasts and Pentecost

Passover is called Pesach in Hebrew. It originated as a result of God sending ten plagues of judgment upon Egypt because of the Pharaoh's refusal to let the Jewish people leave Egypt to worship their God. It also commemorates the Exodus from Egypt by the Jewish people and their protection by God from the ten plagues that were sent upon the Egyptians, their livestock, and their land. It is usually observed during the month of March or April on the Julian calendar and on the 14th day of Nisan on the Jewish calendar. The feast lasts for seven days. The day following Passover, starts on Nisan 15. It is the Feast of Unleavened Bread. This feast is followed by the Feast of First Fruits. This feast lasts from the 16th of Nisan until the 21st of Nisan. The counting of the Omer begins after Passover and continues until Shavuot [Pentecost]. During this time, mature sheaves of the barley harvest are brought to the priest daily for 49 days as a means of receiving God's blessings on the remainder of the harvest.

1. The Feast of Passover [Pesach] and the Passover Lamb

In Exodus 12:3-10, 13, 14 God instructs the congregation of Israel to do the following: Take a lamb for their household on the tenth day of the first month. If the household is too small to consume an entire lamb, then he can share it with his neighbor; according to the number of people and what each person could eat. "Your lamb shall be an unblemished male a year old; you may take it from the sheep or from the goats. 'You shall keep it until the fourteenth day of the same month, then the whole assembly of the congregation of Israel is to kill it at twilight. 'Moreover, they shall take some of the blood and put it on the two doorposts and on the lintel of the houses in which they eat it. 'They shall eat the flesh that same night, roasted with fire, and they shall eat it with unleavened bread and bitter herbs. 'Do not eat any of it raw or boiled at all with water, but rather roasted with fire, both its head and its legs along with its entrails. 'And you shall not leave any of it over until morning, but whatever is left of it until morning, you shall burn with fire. . . 'The blood shall be a sign or you on the houses where you live; and when I see the blood I will pass over you, and no plague will befall you to destroy you when I strike the land of Egypt. 'Now this day will be a memorial to you, and you shall celebrate it as a feast to the Lord; throughout your generations you are to celebrate it as a permanent ordinance.

Why did God want an animal sacrifice when I Samuel 15:22 says: ... "Has the Lord as much delight in burnt offerings and sacrifices as in obeying the voice of the Lord? Behold, to obey is better than sacrifice, and to heed than the fat of rams". The Lord is interested in a contrite spirit and a right attitude toward Him.

The animal sacrifice was a forerunner of the blood sacrifice of Yeshua Jesus for our redemption. The purpose of the blood sacrifice was to build a relationship between Father God and the children of Israel. The life of an animal was considered precious and sacred. Its death was meant not only to draw the Jews closer to God but also to show them how grievous their sins were that God was covering them with blood. Their sacrifice was not meant to be seen as appeasing an angry god like what was done in the pagan system, but was meant to be given to a merciful God who loved them and protected them. It was not about fulfilling a duty because God looks at the heart of man not the works of a man. God wants a covenant relationship with His children based on trust, not a relationship based on fear, distrust, a ritual, or legalism. He wants an inward transformation of the heart. God tells us how He feels in Isaiah 1:11-17. It says: "What are your multiplied sacrifices to Me? Said the Lord; I have had enough of burnt offerings of rams, and the fat of fed cattle; and I take no pleasure in the blood of bulls, lambs, or goats. When you come to appear before Me, who requires of you this trampling of My courts? Bring your worthless offerings no longer; ... new moons and Sabbaths, the calling of assemblies... I hate your new moon festivals and your appointed feasts. They have become a burden to Me; I am weary of bearing them. So when you spread out your hands in prayer, I will not listen. Your hands are covered with blood". God desires a person to have the right attitude toward Him not one of simply going through the motions of a ritual or doing a deed.

For born-again believers in Yeshua Jesus, the three sprinkles of blood, two on the doorposts and one the lintel of the house, are symbolic of the cross of our Lord on Golgotha, "the place of the skull" – John 19:17. Rabbi

Cahn described the three blood sprinkles as one part of two triangles. He said the blood sprinkles form one triangle with their top point on the door lintel, and one sprinkle on each of the sides of the two doorposts. The sides of a second triangle are formed by the two outstretched arms of Messiah on the cross, and the bottom point is formed where His feet were nailed together at the side of His ankles on the bottom of the cross. When one joins the two triangles together, one of the triangles points upward and the other points downward. It is as if God is looking down at man and man is looking up to God. When joined together they form the star of David! It is an interesting note that archeologists have found a bone of a foot with a nail bent in the ankle. This artifact can be seen at The Museum of the Book in Jerusalem, Israel. Some researchers and Bible teachers, including Perry Stone and Rabbi Jonathan Bernis, believe that Yeshua Jesus was actually nailed to a pole, with His arms crossed and nailed over His head on the pole and His ankles nailed on the base of the pole, rather than nailed on a Roman style cross with His arms outstretched. This posture is reminiscent of the image of the bronze serpent that Moses placed on a pole in the wilderness; so if a man was bit by a serpent, when he looked to the bronze serpent on the pole, he lived – Numbers 21:9. It is also a reminder of when Jacob crossed his hands over the heads of the two sons of Joseph in order to bless them – Genesis 48:14. Since the Scripture contains patterns, these two images of a serpent on a pole and of Jacob crossing his hands over the heads of Joseph's sons, may be actual proof of how Yeshua Jesus was nailed to the pole/cross at the time of His crucifixion.

Since Yeshua Jesus was nailed on the pole/cross and died on Passover, it is important to take a closer look at this feast and how it connects with Yeshua our Messiah. First remember that a new day begins at sundown for the Jewish people. With that in mind we will once more return to the book of Exodus, Chapter 12. As we read the text the first thing we notice is that the Hebrews were instructed to roast a lamb without blemish and they could not keep any that was left over until the morning. Why? Because Yeshua, our Messiah, was on the cross for one day and was taken off the cross in the morning after He committed His spirit back to His Father. Second, it was the blood of the lamb on the homes of the Hebrews that saved Father God's people from the plagues of Egypt. It is the blood of Yeshua Jesus that saves all who are redeemed from eternal damnation. Third, it was written that they should roast it all, head, legs and entrails, and so no bone was to be broken. When the Roman soldiers went to break the bones on the legs of those on the cross to hurry their death, they did not break the bones of Messiah because He was already dead. John 19:31-34 describes the fact of Yeshua's death. It says, then the Jews, because it was the day of preparation, so that the bodies would not remain on the cross on the Sabbath [for that Sabbath was a High Holy Day], asked Pilate that their legs might be broken, and that they might be taken away. "So the soldiers came, and broke the legs of the first man and of the other who was crucified with Him; but when coming to Jesus [Yeshua], they saw that He was already dead, they did not break His legs, but one of the soldiers pierced His side with a spear, and immediately blood and water came out".

2. The Feast of Unleavened Bread

Exodus 13:6-7 says, on the seventh day there shall be a feast for the Lord. The Jews call this feast the "Meal of the Messiah". Unleavened bread shall be eaten throughout the seven days; and nothing leavened shall be seen among you, nor shall any leaven be seen among you in all your borders".

Unleavened bread represents the rush to freedom from bondage in Egypt for the Jews. They considered it to be part of the Passover. For the Christians, unleavened bread represents the sinless nature of Messiah who was buried on the first day, Nisan 15, of The Feast of Unleavened Bread. II Corinthians 5: 21 says, "Yeshua knew no sin but He became sin on our behalf so that we could be redeemed. What an incredible love!!

3. Feast of First Fruits

An interesting fact about First Fruits for the Christian is that the Ark rested after the flood of Noah on the same day the resurrection of Yeshua Jesus, Messiah took place.

Leviticus 23:10-12 says: "Speak to the sons of Israel and say to them, 'When you enter the land which I am going to give to you and reap its harvest, then you shall bring in the sheaf of the first fruits of your harvest to the priest. He shall wave the sheaf before the Lord for you to be accepted; on the day after the Sabbath the priest shall wave it. Now on the day when you wave the sheaf, you shall offer a male lamb one year old without defect for a burnt offering to the Lord".

Why did the lamb that was offered as a sacrifice have to be one year old? For the Jewish people, the blood of the lamb placed their name in the Book of Life for one year only, from Yom Kippur to Yom Kippur. Without belief in Yeshua Jesus their redemption was not eternal but temporal, and had to be renewed year after year. The lamb without blemish is a reflection of our Messiah.

This feast was always celebrated on a Sunday. Yeshua's Ascension was on a Sunday. He is the lamb of God and the first fruit of many to come and be given to His Father in heaven.

The Involvement of the Godhead in the Three Spring Feasts

Our God is an amazing God! When we think of the Spring feasts, all three members of the Godhead participated in their fulfillment. Michael Norten points out that, "The Son honored and fulfilled the Feast of Passover by His death [including the Feast of Unleavened Bread which is part of Passover]. The Father honored and fulfilled the Feasts of First Fruits by raising His son Christ from death and the grave. The Holy Spirit honored and fulfilled the Feast of Weeks/Pentecost by His descent fifty days after the resurrection of Christ and indwelling the disciples with His Spirit so they could better minister and proclaim to Gospel to all and tell them that Jesus is; the Son of God, the Messiah, and the Savior of those who believe".

4. Shavuot and Feast of Weeks is also called Pentecost

Shavuot is called the Feast of Weeks by the Jews for it occurs seven weeks after Passover, and on the fiftieth day of the counting of the Omer. An Omer is about a half gallon of grain which was given to the Temple priests from each person's harvest. For the Jews, Shavuot celebrated the giving of the Torah by God. For the born again believer, the fiftieth day known as Pentecost was the day the Christian church was supernaturally born. It is the day the Holy Spirit came down as flames of fire on the heads of Yeshua's disciples and endowed each one with the ability to speak in a previously unknown language. The Holy Spirit enabled the disciples to share the Gospel in strength and power with everyone they encountered. Dr. Chuck Missler believes that the Rapture of the church may take place on Pentecost.

Exodus 19 speaks of the origins of Pentecost as when Moses was on Mount Sinai for forty days to meet with the Lord. There he received the Ten Words [Commandments]. After receiving the Lord's commandments, he walked back down the mountain and into the desert to rejoin the people. It is thought to have taken him ten days to return to the people. Upon his return he unfortunately found celebrating a golden calf they had made. Why were they celebrating a golden calf? This calf was an image of Apis, one of the gods of Egypt. Apparently they had worshipped this god during their captivity in Egypt and did not yet recognize the true God, Hashem, who had freed them from bondage. Instead they attributed their freedom to Moses! God became incensed with the children of Israel at this point because He had commanded them not to create or worship any graven image.

A Brief Overview of the Three Fall Feasts

Leviticus 23:24-25 says: Speak to the sons of Israel, saying, In the seventh month on the first of the month you shall have a rest, a reminder by blowing of trumpets, a holy convocation. You shall not do any laborious work, but you shall present an offering by fire to the Lord.'"

The three Fall feasts have not been fulfilled yet, but we can be certain that Yeshua will fulfill them to the very hour and day at the time of His Second Coming just as He fulfilled the Spring feasts during the time of His First Coming. These Fall Feasts tell born-again believers what will happen in the future. This was announced in Revelation 11:15 as it proclaims: The kingdom of the world has become the kingdom of our Lord and of His Messiah, and He will reign forever and ever!

1. The Feast of Trumpets/Rosh Hashanah/Yom Teruah

Leviticus 23:24 says: Speak to the sons of Israel, saying, 'In the seventh month on the first of the month you shall have a rest, a reminder by blowing of trumpets, a holy convocation.

The Feast of Trumpets, also called Rosh Hashanah and Yom Teruah, is the first of the Fall feasts. It is called "the day of blowing" and it initiates the Ten Days of Awe in which the Jewish people spend ten days of introspection and penitence prior to Yom Kippur. It also represents the civil New Year for the Jewish people. This New Year celebration is signaled by the blowing of trumpets 100 times. Many born again believers believe this feast represents the timing of the Rapture of the church when God Himself will blow the shofar [the last trump] as a signal of the end of the Gentile age. This belief is based on I Corinthians 15:51-53. It says: "Behold, I tell you a mystery; we will not all sleep, but we will all be changed, in a moment, in the twinkling of an eye, at the last trumpet, for the trumpet will sound, and the dead will be raised imperishable, and we will be changed. For this perishable must put on the imperishable, and this mortal must put on immorality".

2. Yom Kippur/Day of Atonement

Leviticus 23:27 says: "On exactly the tenth day of this seventh month is the day of atonement; it shall be a holy convocation [Sabbath] for you, and you shall humble your souls and present an offering by fire to the Lord".

This is the one day of the year the High Priest could enter into the Holy of Holies in the Temple in Jerusalem to offer sacrifices for himself, the Levites, and the nation. Two identical goats were chosen to be part of the sacrifice – one was roasted on the altar before the Lord as a burnt offering, and the other called the Azazel or scapegoat had the sins of the Jewish people symbolically placed on its face and head by the High Priest. After this action was completed the scapegoat, with a red sash around its horns, was taken into the wilderness where it was thrown over a cliff to die. This assured the people that the scapegoat would not return to the city still bearing their sins.

Yom Kippur is the most holy day of the Jewish year. It ends the ten days of repentance, prayer, fasting, renewal, and forgiveness while the Book of Life is open. At the end of Yom Kippur the Book of Life is closed for another year.

To born-again believers, Yeshua Jesus was our sacrificial lamb and atonement. He was sacrificed for our sins when He, who was innocent of sin, was placed on the cross in our place. Just as the priest had to lay his hands on the Azazel, they had to lay their hands on Yeshua Jesus so He could take the sins of the world upon Himself.

3. The Feast of Tabernacles/Booths/Sukkot/Ingathering

Leviticus 23:42-43 says: "You shall live in booths [sukkahs] for seven days; all the native-born in Israel shall live in booths, so that your generations may know that I have the sons of Israel live in booths when I brought them out from the land of Egypt. I am the Lord your God".

This is one of three mandated pilgrimage feasts, Passover, Pentecost, and Tabernacles, when all Jewish males are required to go up to Jerusalem, both prior to the destruction of the Temple in 70 AD and during the Millennial Reign of Yeshua Jesus. The Feast of Tabernacles represents the inauguration of the coming kingdom of Messiah when He will rule over all the earth as King of kings and Lord of Lords. It is when the Lord will pour out His spirit on all flesh and is the only feast in which both the Jews and Gentiles celebrate together as we wait for the coming of Yeshua HaMashiach, the anointed one, Messiah. It is the celebration that marks when all nations of the world will come together to praise the Lord. During this feast, a lulav which is made of palm branches, myrtle, willow, and an etrog [a yellow citrus fruit] are waved in all directions to glorify God. The lulav symbolically shows the Jewish people that no matter where they go, no matter how far their travels take them, God is always there with them.

For the born-again believer, they remember Yeshua's triumphal entry into Jerusalem riding on the back of a donkey on Palm Sunday. As He rode, the people spread leafy palm branches before Him and laid their coats in the road. Those who went in front and those who followed were shouting: "Hosanna!" – Mark 11:8-9, just like the Jews did in the Temple during the Feast of Tabernacles.

A Brief Overview of the Two Additional Feasts: Chanukah and Purim

Chanukkah and Purim are not part of the feasts given to Moses found in ***Leviticus 23*** but are national celebrations that mark freedom from annihilation of the Jewish people by their enemies.

1. The Feast of Chanukah/The Festival of Light

The name Chanukah means "dedication" and refers to the new altar placed in the temple after the Jews defeated the Greek army led by Antiochus IV Epiphanes and his sons in the second century. The story is found in the book of I Macccabees. Antiochus IV Epiphanes, one of the cruelest of all the Seleucian rulers, made a systematic attempt to destroy the Jewish people. He desecrated the Temple by sacrificing a pig on the holy altar and by placing a statue of Zeus on it to be worshipped. He also spread pig's blood on the Torah. He wanted a one world government and a one world Hellenistic-style religion. In his attempt to force the Jews to comply to his commands, a revolt broke out led by Mattisyahu Maccabee, his five sons, and others faithful to God and His covenant. In the end, the Jews defeated the Greek Army and restored their temple. It was rededicated to God on the 25th day of Kislev. On that day the priest found one small undefiled container of oil used to light the Menorah. The oil should have lasted one day, but through a miracle lasted eight days. The small number of believing Jews in this revolt and its consequent success is a reminder that God doesn't require a large number of people in order get His will done on earth.

Yeshua Jesus celebrated Chanukah while on earth - John 10:22-23. This was when He declared Himself to be the Light of the World.

2. The Feast of Purim

Esther 9:22 says: "Because on those days the Jews rid themselves of their enemies, and it was a month which was turned for them from sorrow into gladness and from mourning into a holiday; that they should make them days of feasting and rejoicing and sending portions of food to one another and gifts to the poor".

The background of this feast is found in the Old Testament book of Esther. It is celebrated every year on the fourteenth day of Adar [around our month of March]. Even though God is not mentioned directly, His presence is everywhere in the background of this book. It is one of two miracles singled out by the sages for commemoration by festivals.

The story of Purim took place between 485-465 BC during the reign of King Ahasuerus of Persia. Haman, the Prime Minister to King Ahasuerus, was a vicious anti-Semite and Agagite who wanted to destroy the Jewish people. He was a descendant of Amalek who warred against God's people when they left Egypt. Haman deceived the king and tricked him through fear and deception into signing a decree to destroy all the Jews in Persia. In the end, his plot was foiled and he was hung on the very gallows he had prepared for Mordecai, the uncle of Esther, the Jewish Queen.

Clearly there has been a pattern of evil in the world since the fall of Adam and Eve. Satan tried to tempt Yeshua Jesus by promising to give Him all the nations of the world if He would only bow down to him. The very nature of evil is the desire to be God. Why the focused hatred toward the Jews and Israel throughout the centuries? The answer is simple. The existence of the Jewish people is proof that God exists. Additionally, it was the Jews who brought Messiah Yeshua into the world. Satan hates that God's chosen people live and that Yeshua Jesus, the only begotten Son of God, came to save those who believe in Him. Most of all, Satan can't do anything about God's ultimate plan for His people despite his best efforts! The devil is simply no match for God! The Lord is our only hope and in Him we can trust, both in our present life and for our future. He is the true ruler of the universe He created, not Satan whose pride led to his fall before the creation of the world.

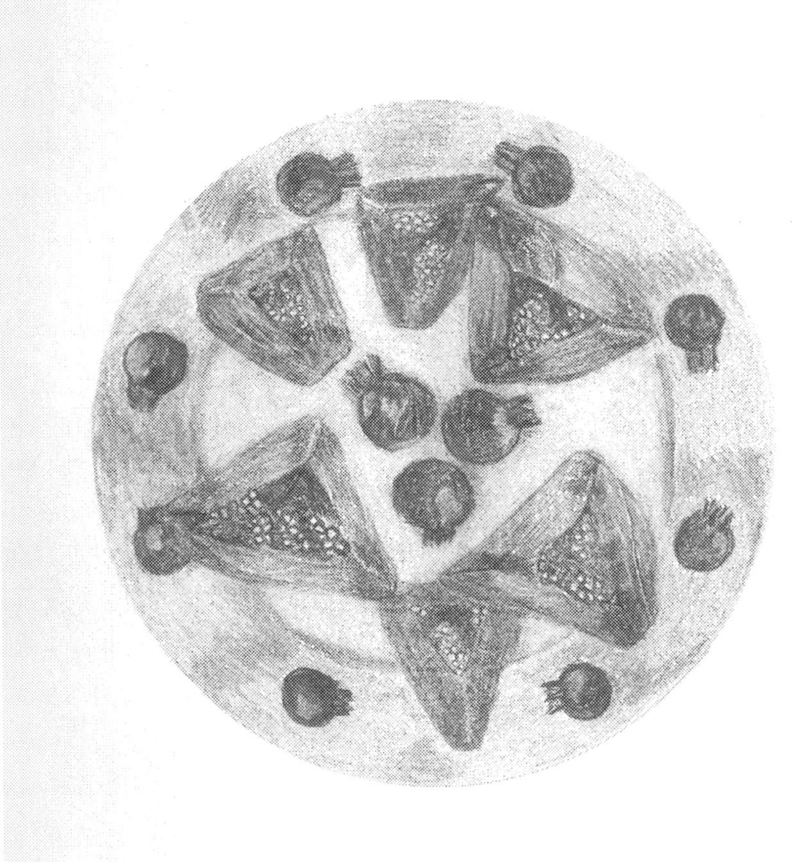

The Feast of Purim

The Feast of Purim is celebrated on the 13th-14th days of Adar (March or early April) beginning at sunset after having fasted the day before. It is one of two feasts that were not given by God to Moses but is a memorial for a significant national event that saved the Jewish people from annihilation. The background of this feast is found in the Old Testament Book of Esther. While God is not mentioned directly in this book, His finger prints are evident as He works behind the scene in every event of the story. The story of Purim reminds us that God is always near to us even when we are in a state of unbelief or when we fail to sense His presence.

Brief History: The Jews, Persia, From King Cyrus to King Ahasuerus

The entire book of Ezra as well as Isaiah 45:1-7 gives us the history of the rebuilding of the Temple in Jerusalem from King Cyrus of Persia [current day Iran] to King Ahasuerus, who is known historically as King Xerxes.

The Jews were taken captive by the Babylonians in 586 BC. Twenty years later, the Persians conquered the Babylonians and took over the Babylonian territory. In the first year of the reign of King Cyrus of Persia, the Lord called upon King Cyrus to write a decree which would give permission for Ezra and the Jewish people to return to Jerusalem and Judea to rebuild the house of the Lord that had been destroyed by Nebuchadnezzar. Cyrus believed that the Lord who had called him by his name before he was born had appointed him to rebuild the Temple in Jerusalem. As a result of this belief, Cyrus had all the articles of silver and gold that had been stolen from the temple by Nebuchadnezzar returned to the Temple. The number of utensils that were counted was 5,400. He also saw to it that all the costs needed to complete the temple were provided for out of the royal treasury from the taxes of the providences. The Jews living in Persia were treated well so many of them did not want to go back to Judea and suffer hardship. As a result, most of the Jews chose to stay in Persia even though it was God's will for them to return to their own land. Despite the ease of living in Persia, a remnant of faithful Jews chose to follow God's will and return to their homeland to rebuild their temple. When the enemies of Judea heard that the Jews were rebuilding their temple, they offered to help. Zerubbabel and Jeshua who headed up the rebuilding process refused their offer since they had nothing in common with the belief of the Jewish followers of the God of Abraham, Isaac and Jacob. As a result of their refusal the people in the land who were enemies of the Jews, frightened the people of Judah and discouraged them from rebuilding their temple. They wrote letters of complaint against the Jews in Jerusalem to King Cyrus. They claimed that the Jews would not pay tribute to the king if the city and temple were rebuilt. These lies continued until the reign of King Darius. In order to find out the truth of the situation, Darius made a search of the archives and found the scroll written by King Cyrus. In the scroll, King Cyrus had given permission for the Temple to be rebuilt on its original site and declared that the Jews were to be given whatever was needed for their sacrifices to the God of heaven. It also decreed if any man violates this edict," he shall be impaled on a timber taken from his house". As a result the elders of the Jews were able to complete the temple on the third day of Adar.

The Story of Esther and Purim

The story of Purim took place between 485-465 BC during the third year of the reign of King Ahasuerus, in Susa, Persia. It recounts God's victory over His enemies who attempted to annihilate the Jews, His chosen people. The key players in the story are: King Ahasuerus, Queen Vashti, Queen Esther, Mordecai. and Haman the wicked Agagite, who was second only to the king in political power in the kingdom.

The story opens with King Ahasuerus' displeasure toward his beautiful wife, Queen Vashti. She had refused his request to display herself wearing only her crown in front of the king's drunken friends during an orgy. Her disobedience made the king very angry, so he called together his cabinet members for their legal advice on how to handle the situation. They suggested that the king give Queen Vashti's position to another woman so other women in the kingdom would not disrespect their husband, and to assure that every man would remain the master of his own house. To save face, the king removed Vashti as his queen and banished her from his kingdom, even though the decision she had made was a correct one. After four years had passed, the king's anger had subsided. He became lonely and remembered Vashti and the decree he had issued against her which could not be reversed. So, he asked his overseers to gather together all of the most beautiful women in the kingdom so he could select another queen from among them. Esther was one of the young women taken to the king's harem. Everyday the king viewed beautiful women from his harem dressed up in lovely raiment and in jewels from the king's treasury. When Esther came before the king she did not request anything from him. This pleased the king and he loved her. So Esther was chosen over all the women and she received grace and favor in the sight of the king.

Esther was the daughter of Mordecai's uncle. Mordecai was a Benjamite, who had raised her since the time of her parent's death. He was a guard for the king. One night Mordecai overhead two of the king's eunuchs, Bigthan and Teresh, planning a plot to kill the king. He immediately went and shared what he had heard with Queen Esther who shared the information with the king in Mordecai's name. The two men were found guilty and hung on gallows. The incident was written in the chronicles of the king and forgotten for a period of time.

Meanwhile, Haman the son of Hammedatha, the Agagite, and a descendant of the evil Amalek was promoted to second in command over the kingdom of King Ahasuerus. He was a very arrogant, narcissistic, and prideful man. When Mordecai refused to bow down to Haman as he passed by, Haman became overwhelmed with a deep, smothering rage toward Mordecai. He became obsessed with the Jews, and began to devise a deceitful plan by which all the Jews in the kingdom would be destroyed. His plan involved deception and trickery. He manipulated the king by misrepresenting the Jews. He told the king that the Jews did not observe the king's laws and were a threat to the kingdom. He asked that they be destroyed. Haman knew if the king would agree to write the decree that it could not be reversed according to the laws of the Medes and Persians. He then attempted to ensure the deal by offering to pay ten thousand talents of silver to whom ever would destroy the Jews and to put the same amount into the king's treasuries. The king naively accepted Haman's offer, and Haman put his plan into motion. First he decided that he needed to cast a Pur [a lot, dice] to determine the best day to annihilate all the Jews in Persia. This belief on how to determine timing for an important action had been passed down from Amalek. According to Pastor Biltz, Amalek's entire philosophy was that there is no God, that all is chance, and that everything is haphazardly dictated by luck. When Haman cast the Pur, it fell on the 13th day of Adar, so Haman sent the decree with the king's seal on it throughout the 127 provinces of the kingdom. The decree declared that all of the Jews were to be destroyed on the 13th of Adar.

Upon hearing the news, Mordecai tore his clothes in grief and loudly wept. He approached Esther and requested her help in saving her people. Esther was fearful at first and hesitated. She felt that her position as Queen in the palace would keep her safe. She knew that she could not go before the King without being summoned by him. If she did as Mordecai asked of her and appeared before the king on her own, she would be killed unless the king raised his golden scepter to her. Mordecai reminded her that God may have put her in the kingdom for such a time as this; that this was her time to speak up. If she chose to avoid the opportunity God had given her to save her people, she would not escape death and God would work elsewhere with someone else. After thinking over what Mordecai had requested of her, Esther asked him to have all the Jews in the kingdom to fast and pray for three days. She told him that she and her handmaidens would also fast for three days and seek God's favor. After the three days she would approach the king. She said, "if I perish, I perish." At that point, she surrendered everything to God and was willing to give up her life so others might live; she put her conscience over her comfort. She had come to understand that some things were more important than one's life. On the third day Esther put on her royal robes and stood in the inner court of the king's palace. When the king saw her he extended his golden scepter and motioned for Esther to come near. When the king asked what her request was up to half of his kingdom, her response was that she wanted the king and Haman to come to a banquet she would prepare for them.

Meanwhile, the king could not sleep so he asked that the book of chronicles be read to him. While they were being read, the incident concerning Mordecai's warning came up. The king realized that Mordecai had not been honored for saving the king's life, so the king planned to honor Mordecai. He asked Haman what he would do for a man the king wants to honor. Haman, thinking it had to be him the king wanted to honor, suggested the king put his royal robe and a crown on the man. In addition, Haman suggested that the king place the honoree on one of the king's horses and parade him through the city. This must have been Haman's fantasy because it was against protocol to touch items that belonged to the king. When the king ordered that these suggestions be followed by Haman for Mordecai, Haman was enraged. After the task was completed, he went home and told his wife and friends how humiliated he felt. His wife and friends told him he would not prevail against Mordecai but he refused to listen. While he was talking, the king's eunuchs arrived to bring Haman to the banquet Esther had prepared.

During the first banquet, Esther's only request to the king was that he and Haman come to another banquet the following evening. Perhaps she did this out of her fear or because she felt it wasn't the proper time to speak, so she reframed. At the second banquet, Esther revealed to the king that she was a Jew and the plot Haman had perpetrated against her people. Haman panicked and when the king stepped out of the room for a moment, he broke palace etiquette and came too close to Esther while she was reclining to eat. Maybe he was begging for his life or perhaps he was being critical and demeaning toward her. In either case, when the king returned and saw what was happening, he became enraged with a white hot anger. He ordered that Haman be hung on the 75' high gallows he had prepared for Mordecai. The king then issued a second decree that allowed the Jews to defend their lives against their enemies on the date Haman had chosen for their destruction, the 13th of Adar. The Jews killed Haman's ten sons and all their enemies. Mordecai was given Haman's position of authority which was second only to the king's. The Jews celebrated the victory God had given to them over the evil decree of Haman, and the 13th of Adar became a day of celebration of feasting, rejoicing, and the sharing of gifts to one another. They call this celebration Purim after the name of the dice that was cast, called a Pur – Esther 9:26. It is to be remembered and celebrated throughout every generation because God knows it is human nature to forget unless one is told to take time to remember. God's people can be attacked but never defeated!!

Who the characters in the story represent

King Ahasuerus was a type of Elohim, the God of justice. He ruled a huge empire, one that stretched from India to Ethiopia; just as God rules the empire of the world. God's decrees of judgment like the decrees of the Medes and Persians can not be revoked [Daniel 6:15]. King Ahasuerus also had the largest Army in the world during his reign just as God has a gigantic Army of angels and believers in heaven.

Queen Vashti was a type of unbeliever. She was the daughter of the pagan king, Cyrus. While she did not know the true God, she was used by Him. It is said in the Talmud that the Angel Gabriel helped secure the salvation of Israel by preventing Vashti from obeying the command of King Ahasuerus to appear at his banquet wearing only her crown. Her decision served to secure the election of Esther as queen in her place. This shows that God can use unbelievers who do not know, honor, or worship Him, to protect His people, and to get His work accomplished on earth.

Queen Esther was a type of Yeshua Jesus, God of compassion and mercy. Her real name was "Hadassah" which means myrtle, the flower which represents love and is used in Jewish weddings. She was chosen to marry King Ahasuerus in 515 B.C. out of the most beautiful women in his kingdom. She interceded for her people just as Yeshua Jesus/Adonai intercedes for those who surrender to Him as Savior. She was willing to lay her life down so others could live. She was courageous, believed God could save her people, and engaged in prayer and fasting to discern God's will.

Mordecai, the Jew, represents the kingship of Messiah. He was a descendant of King Saul. He was exalted and honored because of His selflessness and honesty. He was a man of faith, fasting, and prayer. He was given the honored of riding the King's horse in the city just as Yeshua Jesus was honored as he rode a donkey into the city of Jerusalem on Palm Sunday. He did not seek praise or adoration from others for himself.

The evil Haman is a type of anti-Christ. He was clever, narcissistic, arrogant, and prideful. He was the Prime Minister to King Ahasuerus. He use ruthless in his use of trickery, lies, and manipulation to get what he wanted from the king. He was initially revered by the people. He had great authority and political power, and was the enemy of the Jewish people. He, like Satan, was controlled by his pride. His gallows became his judgment and the instrument of his death once the King realized he had been deceived by Haman.

Haman is a descendant of the evil Amalek and the grandson of Esau, the brother of Jacob. Amalek was the first to fight against the Jewish people after they left Egypt, at a time when they were weak, in an attempt to destroy them. Like a coward, he would pick off the weak ones in the back of the group and kill them first, rather than attacking from the front. Because of Amalek's behavior, the Jews were commanded to "blot out" the name of Amalek. Pastor Mark Biltz has suggested that "God was mocking the beliefs of Amalek in the book of Esther because the philosophy he held. His erroneous beliefs were passed down through the generations in Amalek's family to Haman. The end result of the events in Haman's life proved Amalek and Haman wrong and God right. According to Pastor Mark Biltz the following shows how God works in the world to accomplish His will:

"It just so "happens" that a [God believing] Jew becomes a Queen [to a pagan king].

It just so "happens" that Mordecai hears of a plot to kill the king in a foreign language.

It just so "happens" that the king can't sleep.

It just so "happens" he wants a book read.

It just so "happens" he turns to the very page of Mordecai's saving his life.

It just so "happens" in the middle of the night Haman walks in.

It just so "happens" the king walks in and sees Haman on the bed [where Esther was reclining and eating during the second banquet. This was when Haman's plot to destroy her people, the Jews, was revealed.]

It just so "happens" the gallows created by Haman for Mordecai was just finished".

Did all the events leading up to Haman's death happen just by chance or by divine intervention? Were these occurrences dictated by sheer luck or was God working behind the scenes orchestrating every event?

Pastor Mark Biltz pointed out four items of interest concerning Amalek. "1) the first time Amalek was mentioned in the Scriptures actually occurred over 100 years before he was born! Genesis 14:7-8 shows us Amalek's name is associated with an evil group of people known as the ***Amalek***ites. 2) The second time his name appeared was noted in Genesis 36:12. 3) There were 12,110 Hebrew letters in the Torah between the first and second mention of Amalek's name. 4) This just "happens" to be the exact number of Hebrew letters in the book of Esther"!!

The pattern of evil has existed in the world since the fall of Adam and Eve in the Garden of Eden. Satan uses people to do his dirty work of destroying God's people through his lies, deceptions, ruthlessness, and trickery. He wanted to replace God as the center of the universe as revealed in his famous four "I will's" in Isaiah 14:13-14. Sadly, 1/3 of the angels and many people in every generation have fallen for his deception and treachery. Ezekiel 28:17, 19 gives God's description of Satan as follows: "Your heart was lifted up because of your beauty; You corrupted your wisdom by reason of your splendor. I cast you to the ground; I put you before kings, that they may see you"... and all who know you among the peoples are appalled at you; you have become terrified and you will cease to be forever". It is believed that Lucifer, turned Satan, was the song leader in heaven before his fall. The Scriptures described him as the "son of the morning" and the "bright and morning star" before his fall. He was reputed to be the most beautiful angel, shimmering in the light of God's presence when he was positioned as the anointed cherub over the throne of God. It is almost incomprehensible when one considers how far he fell from God's presence because of his pride. It is no wonder Eve was deceived by his beauty and why God hates pride. It is no wonder Satan hates the people of God, especially when he hears them singing praises to the Lord, for when they do he realizes what he gave up as a result of his rebellion against God.

Another Way to View Esther and Mordecai

It has been suggested by Gordon Franz that both Esther and Mordecai were "in a state of unbelief and outside of the will of God" at the time of Haman's evil decree. As proof they say the Jews were known to have been worshiping different Babylonian and Persian deities since their captivity, rather than worshiping the one true God. Deuteronomy 31:16 confirms the falling away of the children of Israel from the true God and reverting to worshipping false gods when in other lands. Because of this, Franz believes the theme of the book is "God's preservation of His unbelieving people". The proof for Mordecai's unbelief was based on the fact that he was in Persia during the time when he should have been in Jerusalem for Passover, as commanded by God. If Mordecai was a captive in Persia he would not have been allowed to return to Jerusalem for the Passover. The scripture simply tells us he was a guard of the king.

Franz pointed out that the name Mordecai does not have Hebraic origins but comes from Marduk, the name of the pagan deity and that Esther's Persian name "Star" has the same origin as the name of the goddess Ishtar. Again, some scholars fail to mention the fact that it was a common practice for names of captives to be changed based on their position during their captivity. We need only to think of Daniel and his three friends in Daniel 1:7, Joseph in Egypt, and others.

It was also suggested that Mordecai may have had evil motives when he told Esther to keep her ethnicity a secret. While it has been pointed out in the Scripture that Mordecai was the one who suggested to Esther that she keep the fact that she was Jewish a secret, there may have been an important reason to do so. She may have complied with his request for one of several reasons of her own. First, she may have felt she was safe from anti-Semitism as long as she kept her secret, especially since she lived in the Palace as the Queen of the King. Second, she may have felt that the revelation of her ethnicity was in God's hands and a matter of His timing. Third, an angel from God, such as Gabriel, may have kept her silent. Fourth, she may have kept silent simply out of timidity and fear and had no other ulterior motive, especially given the trauma she experienced as a child by the loss of her parents. Fifth, The Scripture does tell us that after she had been asked to speak to the king, Esther said she would first engage in an extended three day fast in order to seek out the will of God – YHWH - as a source of help. This would indicate that Esther was a believer in the true God of her fathers and dependent on Him. Once she decided to speak to the king on behalf of her people, she made the needs of her people personal; and to the Jews she became one of them and their heroine. She no longer felt disconnected from her heritage or ashamed of whom she was.

Finally, it has been insinuated by some that Mordecai was being cunning when he told Esther to keep the fact she was Jewish a secret; that her secret was his ace in his pocket that he would use to blackmail Esther with if she failed to do his bidding by refusing to approach the king on behalf of her people's lives. Thus it was felt that he was not just alerting her of the danger they were in, but if need be, would reveal her secret to the king. There is nothing in the Scripture to suggest that Mordecai was an unloving, unscrupulous scoundrel who wanted to control Esther; therefore these explanations do not fit the Biblical narrative.

Purim and Yeshua Jesus in the New Testament

The Book of John mentions the fact that Yeshua Jesus participated in a feast prior to celebrating Passover. The only feast prior to Passover is Purim. John 5:1-2, 5, 7-9 says: "After these things there was a feast of the Jews, and Jesus went up to Jerusalem. Now there is in Jerusalem by the sheep gate a pool, which is called in Hebrew Bethesda, having five porticoes... 'a man was there who had been ill for thirty-eight years'... and Jesus said to him, "Do you wish to get well?" The sick man answered him, "Sir I have no man to put me into the pool when the water is stirred up, but while I am coming, another steps down before me." Jesus said to Him, "Get up, pickup your pallet and walk". "Immediately the man became well, and picked up his pallet and began to walk". Now it was the Sabbath on that day".

There are several significant things to notice in these verses that indicate this miracle occurred on Purim.

First, we know this miracle occurred during a feast of the Jews. The feast mentioned is believed to have been Purim because it is the only feast that occurs in the Spring before Passover.

Second, it was specifically pointed out that the paralytic man Yeshua Jesus spoke to and healed had been as slave to his ill body for 38 years.

Third, the paralytic was sitting by the sheep gate by a pool that was surrounded by five porches. The number five represents God's grace. It is likely that everyone who went by either saw or knew him since he had been there for so many years hoping to be the first one in the water when it stirred and be healed. It was Yeshua Jesus alone who showed compassion and grace on him. The Complete Jewish Study Bible attributes the stirring of the water in the pool that brought healing to an angel of ADONAI, not a Greek god as many of the people believed.

Historically the Jewish Temple in Jerusalem was believed to have stood near the Shrine of Asclepius, the Greek god of health and healing. This shrine was located near the Pool of Bethesda, which means "house of mercy" in Hebrew. It was a place where acts of mercy and healing toward the sick had taken place at times. It is likely that Yeshua Jesus chose to perform this miracle of healing for the paralytic man here in order to show the people assembled there that His strength and His power were greater than that of the god Asclepius. The paralytic man was obviously hoping for a cure from Asclepius, not from Yeshua, whom he may not have heard of. But it was Yeshua who reached out to him and showed him mercy. At the same time, He showed the people assembled there that He did not need a specific place, an angel, some pagan ritual using sacred snakes, or the "stirring of the water" to heal. He simply said, "Get up, pick up your pallet and walk". This miracle clearly showed the people who Yeshua Jesus was and pointed to His divinity so they would believe in Him, their Messiah. He alone is the one true and holy God. He is our "indescribable gift" – II Corinthians 9:15.

It was also during this time that Yeshua Jesus declared that God is His Father. This, acknowledgment informed the people that He, Yeshua, is equal with God. He also said He was the "Son of God" and the "Son of Man". These claims made the priests and Pharisees very angry and led to their decision to kill Him.

Fourth, Yeshua Jesus presented him with a Purim gift when He told the man to get up and walk; a gift the paralytic man graciously accepted without question.

Fifth, the man's healing occurred on a Sabbath which angered the religious Jews. The healed paralytic man is believed to be the one who told the Jewish leaders that it was Yeshua who healed him.

Why did Yeshua Jesus choose to heal a 38 year old paralytic man?

In addition to showing the people the true source of healing power and strength is Yeshua Jesus, there is another possible explanation for His healing of the paralytic man. Numbers have always had significant meanings in the Scripture and are not there by chance. The Scripture is specific about the age of the man Yeshua Jesus healed. The number thirty-eight is in the Scripture only three times in the Old Testament and once in the New Testament. Each time the number comes up it refers to slavery. In the New Testament it appears in the book of John. The paralytic was enslaved in his body with no one to help him. He desperately needed the grace of Yeshua to heal him and Yeshua Jesus had compassion on him. His healing was a Purim miracle for all to see.

To understand how the number connects with the children of Israel one must add together the numbers representing the sum of two events. First the Scripture says the children of Israel wandered for forty years in the Wilderness after leaving Egypt because of their lack of belief and trust in the true God and the promises He had made to their ancestors. When the twelve spies returned after having spied out the land of Canaan for forty days, the majority of Israelites believed the evil report given by ten of the twelve spies. They feared the Nephilim [giants] who lived in the land and saw themselves as small as grasshoppers instead of trusting what God told them to do – Numbers 13:25-33. Thus they were making their decision on what they had seen with their physical eyes rather than with their spiritual knowledge. As a result, God punished them one year for each day the ten spies were in the land. One year for each of forty days spying in the land equals forty years. As Franz points out, at the time of the report, the Israelites had already spent two years wandering from Egypt to Kadesh Barnea while God was teaching them to trust in the fact that He alone is the one true God rather than the false gods of Egypt they had been worshiping. Thus forty years minus two years they had already spent in the desert equals thirty-eight years. Franz believes that the thirty-eight year old sick man was actually "a picture of the state of Israel". That belief was based on the children of Israel's refusal to trust the Lord and enter into the Promised Land which He had prepared in advance for them to conquer and dwell in. They had once again allowed their fear and unbelief to overtake God's will and promises for them.

Why is such hatred been focused on the Jewish people and toward Israel?

The answer is simple. The answer lies in Satan's hatred toward God's chosen people .

First, the existence of the Jewish people is proof that God exists, is victorious, and that Satan has already lost his battle to be God's replacement regardless of how many people he can seduce into following him and doing his will. The Scripture tells us that he convinced 1/3 of the heavenly host to follow him instead of God!

Second, Messiah Yeshua was brought into the world by God and His appointed earthly Jewish parents. Satan knows he can't do anything about that so he tries to destroy the flesh and blood people of Messiah by using deceptive strategies. The strategies he uses in his attempt to destroy God's people are: annihilation [murder and destroy], assimilation [stop Jews from being Jews and the Christians from being Christians], lies, and deceit.

Third, Satan hates that God's chosen people, both the Jew and the Christian, stand on biblical principles and follow God's law.

Fourth, Satan, like Haman, hates the Jewish people because they will not bow down to him so he wants them destroyed. He wants to replace God and be the ruler of the world.

He says in Isaiah, I will be like the Most High God and raise my throne above the stars of heaven.

Fifth, Satan wants God's people destroyed so Israel will cease to exist. He hates Israel. If there is no Israel then the Millennial Reign of Messiah will not happen. In this day of darkness and evil, the Lord is our only hope; and in Him we must trust, both now as well as in the time of Esther.

The Spirit of Amalek in the World

Hatred toward the Jews and incitement against them has occurred throughout history driven by the spirit of Amalek [Satan]. There have been many national and international leaders with this evil spirit in the world from the time of the Babylonians to current terrorist regimes. That is why the Scriptures say there will be an Amalek in every generation that God will war against. Some of the ancient leaders include: Amalek, the grandson of Esau. Amalek fought against the Jews and killed many of them when he attacked the weak ones in the back of the group as they left Egypt for the Promised land. Amalek was brazen. For him it was not about winning the battle against the Jews but about killing as many Jews as he could. Haman who wanted to be greater than King Ahasuerus and plotted to destroy the Jewish people in Persia [Iran] and Antiochus IV Epiphanes wanted to destroy the Jews through their assimilation into the Greek culture and by death. This was followed by the Roman Empire.

They too hated the Jews and fought against them for failing to do their bidding. They used dispersion to scatter them all over the world.

In 1096 the Jews were called "Christ killers" by the Crusaders who tried to destroy them. In 1147 the Jews in France were frequently massacred. Between 1216 and 1272 the Jews in England were being heavily taxed. Many of them lost their money and their businesses. By 1290 the 3,000 Jews living in England under Edward I were expelled because of jealousy and anti-Semitism. In 1392 100,000 Jews were expelled from France. In the mid-1400's the Jews were blamed for the "Black Death" which destroyed almost half of the world's population. As a result, they were openly persecuted and burned at the stake. In 1421 thousands of Austrian Jews were deported and fled to Poland. In 1449 an outbreak in Toledo, Spain sparked the first persecutory hatred between the old Christians and the new Jewish-Christian converts in Spain. This hatred and mistreatment of the Jews soon spread throughout the entire nation. In the 1500's the Jews saw the rise of Ferdinand and Isabella of Spain. They issued a royal edict that led to the Spanish Inquisition in the late fifteenth century. They sought to search out and punished converts from Judaism who were secretly practicing Jewish beliefs and festivals. They gave the Jews three choices: 1) be true to Catholicism, 2) leave Spain, or 3) be killed. Many left the country and sailed to America in 1492 but many others fled to Poland. Those who could not get out of Spain in time died for their faith. It was estimated by the mid-1600's three-fourths of all Jews lived in Poland. In 1517, the Ottoman Empire took over much of the Middle East, including the land of Israel which they ruled for 400 years until 1917. They were defeated and the land of Israel was once again returned to the Jews after World War I through the Balfour Declaration.

Leaders from the 1930's through the 1940's who attempted to destroy the Jewish people include: Adolph Hitler and his Nazi cohorts, such as Joseph Goebbels, Hermann Goring, Rudolph Hess, and Heinrich Himmler to name a few, who attempted to annihilate the Jewish people using Hitler's "Final Solution" and Joseph Stalin of Russia who followed and outsmarted Vladimir Lenin during World War II. Both Stalin and Hitler's lives ended in self-destruction. On May 14, 1948 the State of Israel was born [a nation born in a day]. One day after declaring statehood, this fledging little nation, no larger than the state of New Jersey, was attacked by the surrounding Muslim nations. Again, with God's help, a miracle took place and the Jews defeated their enemies. Since that time the Jewish people have seen nothing but war as their enemies continue their attempts to destroy the Jewish nation and the people of Israel.

Twenty first century leaders include: Saddam Hussein who was the President of Iraq. He tried to emulate Stalin. He annihilated thousands of people like a modern day Haman. After several years he was located in Baghdad, hiding in a hole in the ground, after being hunted down by the American military. An amazing fact about him was that he was hung on his own gallows; on the same day that Haman was hung on his gallows 2,500 years earlier! He was followed by Gamel Nasser and then by Yasser Arafat, both of whom were Egyptians. Arafat was the first President of the Palestine Liberation Organization [PLO]. He tried to commandeer the land of Israel from the Israelis by claiming they had stolen and occupied Palestinian land. Unfortunately many politicians in the West believed his lies! Mahmoud Abbas took over as President of the PLO after the death of Arafat and continues his policies to this day. Mahmoud Ahmadinejad and Ali Khamenei are two of several more leaders of Iran who have wanted to "wipe Israel off the face of the map"; and the list goes on from here!

In 2002 a group of nations consisting of the United Nations, the European Union, Russia and the U.S. set up what they called the Quartet. Their whole purpose was to try to coerce Israel to give up land to the Palestinians so they could have their own state, even though this plan had failed miserably when Israel gave up the Gaza Strip to the Palestinians. The Palestinians want all the land of Israel. Every attempt at peace only brings war.

God brought a change of leadership to America in 2017 in the person of Donald J. Trump, a type of King Cyrus. As a duly elected President he confirmed a law that was written in the 1950's to move the American embassy from Tel Aviv to Jerusalem, the undivided and eternal capital of Israel. This sent a strong message of support to the Israelis and showed the world once and for all that the land of Israel [Eretz Israel] was given to the Jewish people as their inheritance by God. Soon two other nations followed the American lead: Guatemala in Central America and the Czech Republic in central Europe.

The first terrorists who were unfair to the Jews were mentioned in the Scriptures in Genesis 23:7. They were the Hittites, the sons of Heth. Abraham had approached Ephron the Hittite and inquired about purchasing a burial plot in the cave of Machpelah for his wife Sarah who had just died. Ephron was so greedy that he charged Abraham 400 shekels of silver, over twice what the land was worth. This angered God so much that in the Hebrew language Ephron's name is spelled with the *vav* missing which means he was a very small person in the sight of God or in modern terms, a dirt bag!

Currently ISIS/ISIL, Hamas, Al Qaeda, Hezbollah, and other terrorist groups from Libya, Iraq, Syria, Iran, Lebanon, Turkey, Yemen, Sudan, Pakistan, Somalia, Gaza, and Saudi Arabia all support terrorism and want to destroy both Israel and America. Jewish residents living near the Gaza Strip are in constant danger of terrorist attacks. Hamas builds tunnels into Israel almost daily in their attempt to destroy Israelis. Fortunately the Israeli Defense Forces find the tunnels and destroy them before harm is done. Our President Donald J. Trump requested that most of the people immigrating to America from these terrorist laden countries be placed on a temporary travel ban until the U.S. can figure out an effective way to seriously vet refugees from these areas. The liberals, who are seeking to create and control a one world government, disagree even though the terrorists from these countries use murder, fear, intimidation, horrific brutality and torture to control their own people and others they capture. Often the heinous acts they engage in, such as decapitating the head of a Christian, are shown by video on various news and media outlets around the world; and as long as they can control people by fear, the evil Amalek/satanic spirit will continue to do its work. When a person surrenders to God's spirit the satanic spirit has no hold on them. The Scriptures reveal to us that the spirit of anti-Christ exists in every enemy of Israel and in every generation from the day the Hebrews were freed from their bondage in Egypt to now. Since the United States is also a covenant country, the enemies of God want to destroy it too. Recently the Muslim nation of Turkey has begun attacking Christians and Jews and falsely claiming they are breaking the law. In reality the President of Turkey, Recep Tayyip Erdogan, wants to inhibit the practice of religions other than Islam. He is imprisoning Christians for what he calls "Christianization" which he considers a terrorist act. It is important to remember that God said, "I will utterly put out the remembrance of Amalek from under heaven...The Lord will have war with Amalek from generation to generation" - Exodus 17:13-16

Note: The biblical city of Shushan is believed by many to be Hamadan, Iran. Persian Jews visit this city yearly to see a five hundred old building that is believed to have been built over the burial site of Esther and Mordecai. At this point the site is well maintained but as recent as 2010 has become the focus of threats by radical Muslims who call for its destruction. So far the government is guarding it in its attempt to show the world that they tolerate religions other than Islam. A second possible burial site is located in northern Israel near the Israeli border with Lebanon.

How is Purim celebrated today in Israel?

The Jewish people keep the Feast of Purim in much the same way as they did in the days of Queen Esther. It is held yearly on the 13th of Adar which is usually in the month of March on the Julian calendar. It begins the evening before the Feast of Purim with a fast called the Fast of Esther. In the afternoon service, before Purim, it is customary to give three coins, preferably silver with the number ½ on them, to charity. This is done in memory of the silver half shekels that were given as the Temple tax. In the evening of Purim, the Book of Esther [the Megillah] is read in the synagogue after the nighttime prayers. Each time Mordecai's name is mentioned, everyone says, "Blessed be Mordecai". Each time the name of Haman is mentioned, everyone shouts, boos, stamps their feet, or makes other noises, and says, "Cursed be Haman". This action is in keeping with God's command to "blot out the name of Haman". The next morning, after morning prayers, the Book of Esther is read a second time. Like before, Haman's name is stomped out with noise. After the morning service, everyone goes home and enjoys a festive meal called the Purim Seudah. The families eat specially prepared foods including at least one cooked food and bread, and drink at least one cup of wine –more than usual is better- and eat sweet treats. One specialty treat is a pastry called "Hamentaschen" or "Haman's ears". It is a triangular shaped cookie that is filled with berries or fruits of various kinds. After the meal, the family members exchange gifts with one another, tell stories, dance, and make up humorous plays. Any form of acting out in a wild or dangerous way or any show of sadness is strictly forbidden unless one is in mourning. The emphasis is upon having a good time as it is meant to be a day of feasting and rejoicing.

Young children and adults play games and dress up as the characters in the book of Esther. Some people wear masks of modern day anti-Semitic people such as, Yasser Arafat, Saddam Hussein, or Osama bin Laden. It is a party complete with wine, food and candies of all kinds, but especially with cookies called hamentaschen.

Where does Hamentaschen originate?

Hamentaschen was known to have existed in Europe at the time of the Middle Ages. It is believed that the Ashkenazi Jews from Europe may have adapted this popular cookie for Purim. The pastry has actually been identified by four different things:

1. It is most commonly known in Hebrew as "ozney Haman" or "Haman's Ears". The name derives from the ancient custom of cutting off the ears of a criminal before he is executed.

2. This cookie shaped pastry resembles the three-cornered hat worn by Haman.

3. Some people say it represents the "Fathers of Judaism", Abraham, Isaac, and Jacob. It is believed Haman's power was weakened by the power God gave to the "fathers" so that Esther would have enough strength to save the Jewish people from imminent death.

4. The German word for "pocket" or "pouch" is "tasche" whereas the Hebrew word for pocket or pouch is "tashin". The Jews may have transliterated the German word for their treat since it is made like a pocket to hold the filling.

Why does the Talmud say one is to drink more wine than usual on Purim?

One may question why the Rabbinic sages of the past advised the Jewish people to drink more wine than usual on Purim when they normally suggested moderation. A common comparison in the Talmud was between a sheep, a lion, a pig, and an ape. When a person doesn't drink wine he is quiet like a sheep before it's sheerer. When a person drinks wine in moderation he remains as strong as a lion, When a person has drunk to much wine, he becomes filthy like a pig, and when a person has drunk wine to the point of drunkenness he acts like an ape - speaking obscenities and blind to his own inappropriate actions. Another common saying was 'when wine enters, sense goes out; when wine enters, the secret comes out'. The Old Testament Scripture also warns of drunkenness in Proverbs 23:29-35. First it asks questions, "Who has woe? Who has sorrow? Who has contentions? Who has complaining? Who has wounds without cause? Who has redness of eyes"? The Scripture then answers these questions. It says, "Those who linger long over wine, those who go to taste mixed wine". Then it clearly gives a warning, "Do not look on the wine when it is red, when it sparkles in the cup, when it goes down smoothly; at the last it bites like a serpent and stings like a viper. Your eyes will see strange things, and your mind will utter perverse things. Finally the Scriptures tell what will occur if one drinks to the point of drunkenness. It describes the person as follows: "And you will be like one who lies down in the middle of the sea, or like one who lies down on the top of a mast, They struck me, but I did not become ill; they beat me, but I did not know it. When shall I awake? I will seek another drink." This is an excellent description of addiction to alcohol.

The drinking of wine is significant because it is linked to many of the events that are related to Purim. It is said to bring happiness to one's heart. The Scriptures tell us that King Ahasuerus and his friends were engaged in a drunken orgy which ended with the banishment of Queen Vashti from the palace. Her banishment paved the way for Esther to become Queen. We can assume that Esther served wine at the two banquets she prepared for the king and Haman, just prior to Haman's being hung on his own gallows. For many people who choose to over indulge, a higher level of anger surfaces that is normally kept in check. With this fact in mind, the amount of wine consumed during the banquet likely caused the king to get more angry than usual; especially when he returned from stepping outside the room for a moment and upon his return saw that Haman had broken protocol by coming to close to Esther. This intoxicated behavior combined with Esther's account of Haman's deception and treachery likely lowered the king's inhibitions and further led to Haman's prompt death.

The Scripture says that the Jewish people celebrated their victory over their destruction by feasting. The Hebrew word for feasting gives us insight into how they celebrated. The word for feasting means bread, cooked food, and drinking wine. The Rabbinic Sages therefore encouraged the Jewish people to drink more wine than usual on Purim as part of their feasting because wine generates warm feelings of happiness. This is contrary to the usual warnings that discouraged over-indulgence for fear that persons who engage in this behavior will sin.

How Purim is celebrated at El Shaddai Ministries

Purim was celebrated on March 01, 2018 at El Shaddai Ministries. The first item on the agenda was a song about Purim by the musical group known as the Maccabeats. It was upbeat and joyful, clearly demonstrating all the items that are part of a Purim celebration. After the song, several members of the church put on a short play that told the story of Purim. Then Pastor Biltz, in a jester's hat, and three additional members of the congregation shared the reading from of the story of Esther in the Scriptures. Some adults and many children of various ages were dressed up in various costumes of characters in the Purim story, which is customary to do on Purim. The celebration is similar to the American holiday of Halloween without the occult trappings. At the end of the reading, everyone who had dressed up in a costume was given a candy treat.

A Personal Story

As a child, the Book of Esther was one of my favorite Bible stories. While in elementary, school I was given a series of beautifully illustrated, paperback picture story books, from the Bible. I never tired of reading them over and over again. I would find myself caught up in the mystery of Esther's life and would marvel at how God worked all things out for good, regardless of the circumstances that surrounded her. As I grew older and put away what I considered to be childish things, the picture story books were given to others. Time went by and I forgot about the picture story book of Esther. God seemed to be far away. Later in my adult life I returned to the story of Esther. I realized the very essence of the story is a demonstration of the importance of faith in God and His faithfulness toward those who surrender their lives and will to Him.

The Purim events reveal the supernatural hand of God working in the background of the lives of His people. He has done this at various junctures in human history since He called Abraham out of the land of Ur to follow Him.

ישוע הנצרת והמלך היהודים

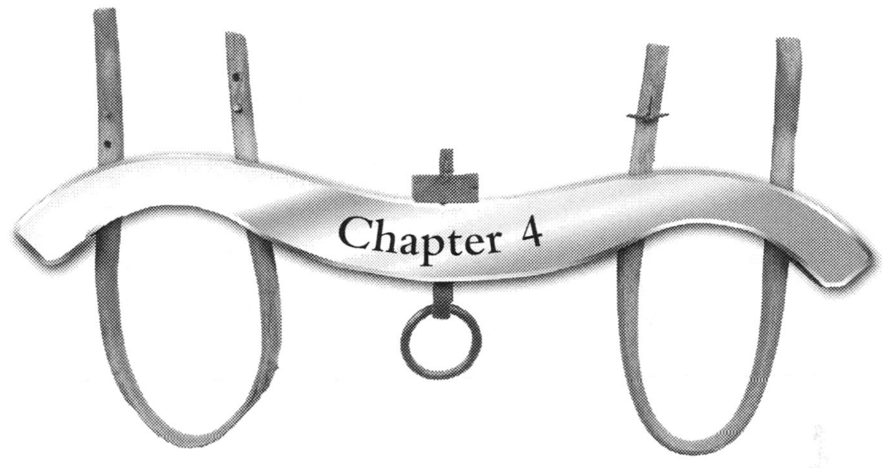

Chapter 4

The Feast of Passover

Passover is called Pesach which means "exempt" in Hebrew. It is the first of the Spring Feasts that were fulfilled by Yeshua at His first coming. It has been estimated that 250,000 lambs were killed at the Temple on Passover. Using one quart of blood per lamb as a measure, 62,500 gallons or 1,100 fifty-five gallon barrels of blood was shed on Passover. That equates to 55 gallon barrels of blood, according to Pastor Biltz. Often 10 people shared one lamb. To the Egyptians, the killing of a lamb was a desecration of their religion. They worshiped the ram at the apex of its strength in the heavens. The Passover sacrifice was a direct challenge to the gods of Egypt. Its theme is human freedom and worship to God.

To the Jews: Passover is about God's deliverance of the Jewish people from bondage in Egypt. When the death angel went throughout Egypt killing the first born of man and livestock, the Jews were untouched because of the blood of the lamb on the door posts and lintel of their homes. The blood of the Passover lamb brought life, freedom, and forgiveness to the Jewish people.

To the Christians: For born-again believers in Yeshua, Passover reminds us of His death on the cross, burial in a rich man's tomb, and resurrection from the dead on the third day.

Historical records indicate that Yeshua's triumphant entry into Jerusalem was on the tenth of Nisan, or March 30, AD 33 on the Julian calendar. On the fourteenth of Nisan between 3:00-5:00 pm the lambs were being sacrificed in the Temple. It was at this very same time that Yeshua [means salvation in Hebrew] was being crucified on the cross at the place of the skull on Golgotha. Michael Norten wrote: "Thus the sacrificing of the Paschal lambs at the temple corresponds to the time of Messiah's death at the ninth hour, 3:00 p.m." the time of the evening sacrifice. Dr. Chuck Missler pointed out that, "God speaks of Israel from this point on as His firstborn".

The Old Testament Historical Viewpoint of Passover

The story of Passover is found in the Old Testament books of Exodus and Leviticus. The historical background however, leading up to the Passover, actually begins in Genesis with Joseph, the favorite son of Jacob who was sold by his brothers out of their jealousy of him and sold as a slave in Egypt. When the famine came and people were starving, Joseph's brothers came to Egypt to buy food for their families. Joseph recognized them and later brought his father, brothers, their families and flocks and herds to reside in Goshen in the land of Egypt so they could be taken care of. Many years passed. The children of Israel and their livestock were fruitful and multiplied in number. Joseph died at 110 years old, fifty-six years after the death of Jacob. Afterwards, a problem arose for the children of Israel when a new pharaoh began to rule. Exodus l: 8 says, "Now a new king arose over Egypt, who did not know Joseph". To understand how this became a huge problem for the Hebrews, one must look back into history to a period around the middle of the eighteenth century BC. At that time, Egypt had been infiltrated by a tribal people known as the Hyksos, whose name meant "rulers of foreign lands". They settled in the northern part of Egypt. Pastor Biltz described the Hyksos as "a conglomeration of ethnic groups among whom Semites predominated". Around 1630 BC they seized power, and ruled Egypt until 1521 BC. They introduced the horse and chariot, improved battle axes, and advanced fortification techniques into Egypt. They also knew Joseph. When the Egyptian pharaoh regained control of Egypt, he didn't know who Joseph was or how he had saved the Egyptian people from starvation. Thus when the new Egyptian pharaoh saw the numbers of the children of Israel he became concerned that they were "more and mightier than we", and feared that he might lose his power to another ruler of Egypt, so he came up with what he considered to be an effective solution. Exodus 1: 10 said: "Come, let us deal wisely with them, or else they will multiply and in the event of war, they will also join themselves to those who hate us, and fight against us and depart from the land." His plan was that all the male babies born of the children of Israel were to be thrown like garbage into the Nile River and drowned. When Yochebed, the wife of Amram, gave birth to their son Moses, they could see he was a healthy child so they hid him out of sight for three months.

The Scripture says when they could hide him no longer she took a wicker basket and covered it over with tar and pitch like the ark of Noah. Then she put the child into it and set it among the reeds by the bank of the Nile – Exodus 2:2-3. The pharaoh's daughter took him out of the river when she heard him cry and raised him as her own son. She named him Moses because "she drew him out of the water" – Exodus 2:10. Moses grew up knowing he was a Hebrew and one day he saw an Egyptian beating a Hebrew slave. He become so infuriated that he killed the Egyptian. When the Pharaoh heard what happened, he tried to kill Moses. As a result, Moses fled to Midian. Years later, Moses was approached by the Lord and given powers and instructions. He was told, in Exodus 4: 21: ... "When you go back to Egypt see that you perform before Pharaoh all the wonders which I have put in your power; but I will harden his heart so that he will not let the people go" [to worship Me]. One might wonder at this juncture, why would God harden the Pharaoh's heart? To understand this, one must understand the meaning in the Hebrew language. The Pharaoh made his own heart hardened through his own stubbornness; God just strengthened it so he could continue the battle.

Exodus 5:2 gives us further insight into Pharaoh's refusal to let the children of Israel go to serve and worship God [on Yom Kippur]. When Moses requested that the children of Israel be let go to worship their God, the Pharaoh asked three questions to Moses. 1) Who is the Lord? 2) Why should I obey His voice and 3) Why should I let Israel go? Pastor Mark Biltz explained that by asking these three questions, "the Pharaoh was challenging first, God's existence as Father; second, the Pharaoh is challenging God's concern for the world and the providence of the Son; and third, the Pharaoh is challenging God's ability to intervene, His omnipotence, His Holy Spirit. We could say in short that the Pharaoh was challenging God's existence, God's concern, and God's ability". As a result of these challenges, according to Biltz, the ten plagues were sent upon Egypt as an answer the Pharaoh's three questions. He taught "the first question was answered by plagues 1-3; the second question was answered by plagues 4-6, and the third question was answered by plagues 7-9, and then sadly for Egypt came plague 10. Plagues number 1, 4, and 7 occurred in the morning; plagues 5, 6, and 8 say "go to Pharaoh"; and plagues 2, 3, and 9 give no warning; and plague 10 was the last plague. Plagues 5, 6, and 8 have the words "go to Pharaoh" in English. Pastor Biltz says this actually means something different in Hebrew. The Hebrew word "Bo" means "come". Therefore God does not tell Moses to "go to Pharaoh" but to "come to Pharaoh", meaning 'come along with Me to Pharaoh'". Plague 10 concerns the death of the firstborn. It had a warning attached to it, but in each case, the plagues do not affect the children of Israel. Exodus 11:4-5, 7 shows how the Lord separates His people from those of the world [Egypt]. It says ... "Thus says the Lord, 'About midnight I am going out into the midst of Egypt, and all the firstborn in the land of Egypt shall die, from the firstborn of the Pharaoh who sits on his throne, even to the firstborn of the slave girl who is behind the millstones; all the firstborn of the cattle as well...But against any of the sons of Israel a dog will not even bark, whether against man or beast, that you may understand how the Lord makes a distinction between Egypt and Israel'.

The gods of Egypt and the Ten Plagues

The gods of Egypt and the ten plagues have been outlined by several pastors as follows:

1. Plague of blood – Hapi was the Nile god. So God had the Nile turn into blood. This showed the death of this god.
2. Plague of Frogs – Heqet was the frog goddess. Because the Egyptians saw that there were many frogs, as appearing from the Nile, they associated the frog with fertility and resurrection.
3. Plague of dust into Lice. Geb was the god of the earth. Earthquakes were believed to be the laughter of Geb.

4. Plague of Insects – Shu was the god of dry air, wind and atmosphere and one who held the sky off of the earth allowing life to flourish in Egypt with his breath of life. So God sent swarms of flies.
5. Plague of the Death of Livestock - Apis was a protector of livestock. So God killed the livestock of the Egyptians.
6. Plague of Boils – Heka was the god of magic and medicine. To the ancient Egyptians they were one and the same. A healer was a man whose tools were a magic staff and a knife. So God sent painful boils on the skin. Some scholars believe that this plague was actually the bubonic plague. Some people believe this was the bubonic plague.
7. Plague of Hailstones – Nut was the god of the firmament who protected man from the heavens. So God sent hailstones. The hailstones destroyed the barley because it was at its most vulnerable stage of development - the stage of Aviv. Thus the stalks and the young seeds were both destroyed.
8. Plague of Locust – Min was the god of vegetation and fertility. Egyptians Harvest Festival was a celebration of the spring-time harvest. So God sent locust that ate up all the vegetation of the Egyptians.
9. Plague of Darkness – Ra was the Egyptians sun god who brought life. So God sent a thick, pitch black darkness upon the land of Egypt for three days. It was so dark it was like a darkness that could be felt. It was so black that the Egyptians could not see one from another, neither did one of them rise up out of his place for three days.
10. Plague of the death of the Firstborn – Amon-Ra was a ram god. He was believed to have been the creator/maker of man. The true God showed the Egyptians that their god was a false god by not only killing the first born of man and beast, but also the lambs they worshipped as divine.

We might ask, why the Lord chose to kill all the firstborn children of the Egyptians and the firstborn of their animals? We must remember that it is the firstborn who carries all their parent's genes and values into the next generation. The Egyptians had been sacrificing to their angry gods for generations in an attempt to appease them. They did not believe in or know who the true God was; His power, His holiness, His love, or in His mercy. They had to learn the hard way by suffering the consequences for their disobedience, and experiencing His judgment.

In ancient cultures people instinctively sensed the need for someone or something higher than themselves to survive, so the pagan system of sacrifices was established. The pagan system used sacrifices as bribes. It was an attempt to make their gods happy and for their gods to bless them. Their ultimate sacrifice was their children. In a sense, it was a type of fire insurance! People today still don't understand God's sacrificial system. They continue to look at it through pagan eyes rather than through the eyes of God's grace and love. In essence, the sacrificial system that God created tells us that God is in charge, not us, and in His love He gave sinful man a way to be forgiven and redeemed. All the true God wants from His people is a broken spirit and a contrite heart ... and then offerings to cover their sins – Psalms 51:16-17, 19.

The First Passover: Preparing the Passover Lamb

Exodus 12 speaks of the Passover Lamb and how to prepare it. The Lord knew the children of Israel would be leaving Egypt in a hurry the next day on Nisan 14, so they were to follow His instructions carefully and completely. They were to eat it with their loins girded, sandals on their feet, and their staff in their hand; and shall eat it in haste. What they did not know was that on this very night, with the death of the firstborn, is a pattern that would be followed exactly by Yeshua the Jewish Messiah thousands of years later.

The procedure was to be as follows: First, each family was to select a perfect lamb on the 10th day of Nisan; one that was one year old and without a spot or blemish. They would then take it home where it was treated like a member of the family for four days. On the 14th of Nisan, the little lamb was slain at twilight. The father of the house was to take some of the blood of the lamb and place it on the doorposts and lintel of the house in which it was eaten. The blood was a sign of their covenant with God who would protect them from the death angel. The lamb was to be roasted on a spit so to avoid breaking a single bone and eaten by the family [or families if more than one family was eating it together] that evening. Nothing could be saved for the next day but if something was left over, it was burnt with fire. And you shall eat it in this manner: with your loins girded, your sandals on your feet, and your staff in your hand; and you shall eat it in haste – for it is the Lord's Passover. Exodus 12:13 says: 'The blood shall be a sign for you on the houses where you live; and when I see the blood I will pass over you, and no plague will befall you to destroy you when I strike the land of Egypt. It was as if God Himself was standing in the doorway of their homes protecting them from harm as He executed judgment against both man and beast of Egypt and all the gods of Egypt.

Passover Preparations in Ancient Jerusalem

Both Ceil and Moishe Rosen and Perry Stone described what it was like in the time of Yeshua Jesus to be in the City of Jerusalem at Passover.

The city of Jerusalem normally had about 600,000 permanent residents at the time of Yeshua Jesus and the Passover Feast. The houses had been thoroughly cleaned and were free of all leaven. Everywhere excitement was building. When the day of the Passover arrived, the population had grown to over two million! Pilgrims came from far away nations, often several weeks in advance, to celebrate the feast, as commanded in the Torah. Frequently families would be invited to sleep in the homes of complete strangers for the week. As the population grew and lodgings became scarce, many people would take refuge in a nearby cave for the night. The Jews at that time, however, would bury their dead in nearby caves and place a large rock at the entrance. Therefore as part of the preparation for Passover, the local people would whitewash the stones that covered the front of the burial cave. This was done to warn strangers so they would not mistake a burial cave for an empty cave. If visitors accidentally slept in a burial cave, they would become unclean. If they were unclean, they would be unable to participate in the feast because it would take a week to go through a ritual purification of one's body after being under the same roof with a dead body, or touching a dead body.

Yeshua Jesus was referring to such a whitewashed tomb in Matthew 23:27-28 when He spoke about the self-righteousness of the scribes and Pharisees. He said, "Woe to you, scribes and Pharisees, hypocrites! For you are the whitewashed tombs which on the outside appear beautiful, but inside they are full of dead men's bones and all uncleanness." So you too, outwardly appear righteous to men, but inwardly you are full of hypocrisy and lawlessness".

Passover was a joyful, noisy, and exciting time in Jerusalem. Since people came from far away countries to celebrate the feast, they brought with them many things to sell. The marketplace was full of all kinds of familiar and unfamiliar items and foods. In addition Ceil and Moishe Rosen said that Passover in Jerusalem was also "a time for making business deals, and a time for servants who had made the decision to undergo the ritual which would indenture them for life to their masters' households". It was a time of reconnecting with family members one hadn't seen for a time and a time to catch up on news and scandals. The wonderful aroma of smoke from the burnt sacrifices in the Temple filled the air.

People brought their lambs to be sacrificed to the priests for inspection. The lambs had to be the prescribed age and completely healthy, without a spot or a blemish to be accepted. The problem was that the priests were dishonest and as a result usually found something wrong with the lambs when nothing was actually wrong. This caused hardship for many who could not afford to purchase a lamb at the temple that the priests had certified as perfect. For people of means, they simply bought another lamb for the high price as demanded. This type of disgraceful behavior by the priests toward the people caused Yeshua Jesus to become so angry that He overturned the tables of the moneychangers in the temple. Luke 19:46 tells us the words Yeshua Jesus said to them. He said, "It is written, 'And My house shall be a house of prayer', but you have made it a robbers' den".

The Passover Shini

The Passover Shini is described in Numbers 9:1-13 and elaborated on by Perry Stone. A problem arose when some people who wanted to attend the Passover as scheduled on Nisan 14 could not because they were unclean. As a result, they went to Moses and Aaron and said, "Though we are unclean because of the dead person, why are we restrained from presenting the offering of the Lord at its appointed time among the sons of Israel?"- Numbers 9:7. The Scripture says that Moses went and inquired of the Lord about this situation and the Lord then spoke to Moses saying: "Speak to the sons of Israel, saying, 'If any one of you or of your generations becomes unclean because of a dead person, or is on a distant journey, he may, however observe the Passover to the Lord...on the second month on the fourteenth day at twilight – Numbers 9: 10-11.

Why was this response by the Lord important? Perry Stone of Manna-Fest Ministries has interpreted this to mean that "someone who is defiled gets a second chance, but someone who is not defiled but neglects the Passover bares his own sin". In essence this means our God is a God of second chances! He is not looking for a way to destroy us but He desires to help us, loves us, and wants to bless us. These things He gives to us freely. He only asks that we love Him and follow His instructions so we can live a pure and holy life.

There were three types of people who did not participate in Passover on Nisan 14. All were allowed to participate in a Passover Shini but there was one group of persons who willfully chose not to participate in either Passover opportunity.

1. The first group allowed to participate in the Passover Shini were those Josephus recorded were unclean on Nisan 14 because they had "leprosy or the gonorrhea, or women that had their monthly courses [menstrual cycles] or such as are otherwise polluted" ... and those, "greedy for gain", who had touched dead bodies as they searched for treasures". Stone says, "This represents those persons who are living in the flesh".
2. The second group who were permitted to attend the Passover Shini was those who had come on a distant journey from remote places. Stone says, "This represents people who were raised in the faith as children but reject and won't honor the blood of the Lamb".
3. The third group simply chose not to attend Passover on Nisan 14 or on the Passover Shini but were not unclean or on a long journey. Stone explained that this group "represents people who know about God but chose not to celebrate and sacrifice at the feast". They will but cut off from of Israel;

The second chance exception does not apply to someone who is not unclean but intentionally chooses not attend Passover on the date initially required. So if one of the children of Israel willfully chose to ignore the Passover on Nisan 14, the scripture says that that man will bear his own sin.

Preparing the Pascal Lamb

The people who were to slaughter the Pascal lambs were divided into three groups. The first group entered the temple and when it was full they closed the doors of the Temple Court. The shofar was then sounded – first the tekiah, then teruah, and then the tekiah again. Groups of priests lined up in alternating rows holding rounded basins. Those holding silver basins were in one row and those holding gold basins were in another row. The rounded shaped bottom of the basins kept the blood from congealing and kept the priests from setting them down and accidentally spilling the blood they contained.

An Israelite slaughtered his lamb by cutting its jugular which led to a quick and nearly painless death. The blood was respectively drained out of the animal and the priest caught the blood in a basin. The priest next to him took the basin and handed it to the priest next to him. The one closest to the altar emptied the basin of blood against the base of the altar. The Israelite then hung his lamb up on one of the iron hooks located on the walls to cut it into pieces. They carefully removed the sacred parts and put them in a tray. These parts were given to the priest who burned them on the altar as a sacrifice to God. This procedure was performed three times, or as many times as necessary, as the Levites chanted the Hallel – Psalms 113-118.

The Ten Symbolic Items in the Passover Meal

Exodus 12:14 says: "Now this day will be a memorial to you, and you shall celebrate it as a feast to the Lord; throughout your generations you are to celebrate it as a permanent ordinance".

In today's celebration, the removal of leaven from the house is a symbolic search to remove all sin. The meal consists of four cups of wine, a Seder plate that contains ceremonial food items, a large family meal, readings, prayers, songs, and praise to the Lord.

To the Jews: Each item on the Seder plate represents part of the Passover story.

To the Christian: each item is a reminder of Messiah and His sacrifice for our redemption/atonement.

Lamb/Shank bone: **To the Jews:** It represents the Pascal lamb that was sacrificed on the evening God delivered them from Egypt.

To the Christians: It represents Yeshua Jesus, the Lamb of God, who was sacrificed for the sins of the world.

Bitter herbs (maror/horseradish): **To the Jews:** It represents the bitterness and misery of slavery in Egypt.

To the Christians: It represents the sorrow we feel for our sins that Yeshua took upon Himself by shedding His blood on the cross.

Charoset (A paste): **To the Jews:** It represents the mortar and bricks they made out of straw and clay for the Pharaoh

To the Christians: It represents forgiveness of our sins and the joy we feel because of our salvation.

Salt water: **To the Jews:** Represents the tears shed as a result of Egyptian slavery.

To the Christians: Represents how Yeshua Jesus, our Savior, turned our tears into joy and washed us clean with His blood. To the redeemed the bowl of saltwater is symbolically like a mikveh in which one purifies himself by dipping his hand into it.

Roasted egg: **To the Jews**: It is simply a holiday offering.

To the Christians: It represents new life in Yeshua Jesus and the eternity we will spend with Him in heaven.

Parsley (Karpas, stems of romaine lettuce): **To the Jews:** Parsley is dipped in salt water to remind them of the sadness of slavery, the tears they shed while slaves in Egypt. It also represents the hyssop that was used to place the blood on the doorpost and lintels of Jewish homes in Egypt to protect them from the death angel in Egypt during the plagues.

To the Christians: When the parsley is put into the saltwater it represents the hyssop and blood that gave us eternal life

Matzah: To the Jews: The unleavened bread is called the Bread of Affliction. It is reminder of how their ancestors left Egypt in haste.

To the Christians: It represents the sinless body of Yeshua Jesus. It is the bread of life for all who believe in Him and call upon Him as their Messiah, Redeemer, and Lord.

Wine: To the Jews: It symbolizes the lamb's blood on the doorposts and lintels in Egypt on the night of the tenth plague.

To the Christians: It symbolizes the blood of Yeshua; and the new life we have in Him.

Elijah's Cup: **To the Jews:** A decorative cup is set out for Elijah. Barry Rubin declared, "It has been our hope that Elijah would come at Passover and announce the Messiah, the Son of David". The background for this hope is found in Malachi 4:5.

To the Christians: This cup represents the future and the return of Messiah Yeshua when He will rule and reign on the Earth. Passover is all about Yeshua; His life, His death, His sorrow, His power and His redemption of His people.

The Four Cups of Passover

To the Jews: wine represents the blood of the lamb placed on the doorposts and lintel of their homes in Egypt the night they were passed over by the death angel. The blood saved their first born children and livestock as the death angel went throughout Egypt killing the first born child and the first born of the livestock among the Egyptians.

To the Christians: wine represents the blood of Yeshua Jesus shed for our sins and our redemption.

Scripturally the four cups of Passover represent the four "I-wills" by God found in Exodus 6:6-7. God speaks to Moses and says: "Say, therefore, to the sons of Israel, 'I am the Lord, and I will bring you out from under the burdens of the Egyptians, and I will deliver you from their bondage. I will also redeem you with an outstretched arm and with great judgments. Then I will take you for My people, and I will be your God; and you shall know that I am the Lord your God, who brought you out from under the burdens of the Egyptians".

FIRST: I AM the Lord. I will bring you out from under the burdens of the Egyptians. This is called the cup of ***SANCTIFICATION.*** This means we are to be set apart from the burdens of the world. This is when the Afikoman, a piece of matzah, is broken into three pieces. Afikoman means "I came" in Hebrew. The middle piece is wrapped in a white cloth and hidden for a child to find later in the Passover celebration. Everyone eats a piece of the Afikoman. The child who finds the hidden piece is given a gift – just like when the bridegroom sends a gift to his bride while she waits for him to return for her.

And when He had taken a cup and given thanks, He said, "Take this and share it among yourselves"– Luke 22:17. Yeshua is the Afikoman, broken for us, placed between two thieves on the cross, buried in a borrowed tomb, and resurrected after the third day. This cup represents redemption by Yeshua alone and that we can never redeem ourselves.

SECOND: I will rid you out of their bondage. This is called the cup of ***DELIVERANCE.*** It means that the chains that held you in bondage to this world are now broken.

During the Seder meal Yeshua said, "But behold, the hand of the one betraying Me is with Mine on the table" – Luke 22:21. This is the point where Yeshua Jesus indicated that He would be betrayed by Judas Iscariot. Judas then leaves the room.

THIRD: I will redeem you with an outstretched arm and with great judgments. This is called the cup of ***REDEMPTION.*** Yeshua has paid the price for our redemption by His outstretched arms. Born-again believers call this cup "Communion". He took the cup after they had eaten, saying, "This cup which is poured out for you is the new covenant of My blood" – Luke 22:20.

FOURTH: I will take you for My people and I will be to your God. This is the cup of ***ACCEPTANCE.*** The redeemed of the Lord thank Him for accepting us into His family and welcome Him into our hearts.

FIFTH: Some do not count this cup as a fifth cup in the meal. It is called the cup of Elijah, and is a cup of praise for all God has done. Religious Jews leave a chair at their table for Elijah. If it remains empty, they believe they have to wait another year for their Messiah and His redemption. Messiah Yeshua is waiting for the Jewish people to acknowledge Him as their Lord and Savior before He will return. Until then, Messiah Yeshua will not drink the fourth cup. The Scripture says, "For I say to you, I will not drink of the fruit of the vine from now on until the kingdom of God comes" – Luke 22:18.

Yeshua Jesus at the Passover and the Last Supper

Yeshua Jesus instructed Peter and John to prepare the Passover Seder. They found the place to share the Passover together [the Upper Room] and prepared the meal as Yeshua had requested. Ceil and Moishe Rosen describe how "on the eve of His death, He showed them [His disciples] the full meaning and symbolism of the Passover memorial". He started with the Kiddush prayer of thanks and sanctification. He then poured the first cup of wine. He humbly washed His disciple's feet. Afterwards, He dipped the matzah into the salt water. This was when Yeshua predicted His betrayal. The disciples asked Yeshua, who will betray you? Yeshua responds: That is the one for whom I shall dip the morsel and give it to him...he dipped the morsel and gave it to Judas.... John 13: 21-26. John 13:27 tells us: "after the morsel, Satan then entered into him" [Judas].

Therefore Jesus [Yeshua] said to him, "What you do, do quickly". Verse 30 says: "So after receiving the morsel he went out immediately; and it was night" and the third cup of wine was poured.

After the Passover lamb was eaten, the disciples drank the third cup of wine. They recited the second part of the Hallel Psalm and the fourth cup of wine was poured and the final blessing for the meal was said. Normally at this point, the meal is complete, but this was where Yeshua Jesus broke from tradition, and instituted a new memorial called "Communion" or "The Lord's Supper". It is described in I Corinthians 11:23-24. Yeshua used the Afikoman which was the center piece of matzah that had been wrapped in a white cloth and hidden, to represent His body and the wine to represent His blood. After this, Matthew 26:36 tells us that Yeshua and His disciples went out to the Mount of Olives to a place called Gethsemane.

The Scripture tell us that Judas felt remorse after he had betrayed Yeshua Jesus with a kiss when he saw that the Chief Priest and elders had condemned Yeshua. So, he tried to return the thirty pieces of silver he had been paid to betray Yeshua to them. Since the priest refused to take the coins back, Judas threw them on the sanctuary floor and left. At this point Matthew 27:5 simply records that Judas went away and hanged himself. Here the story gets interesting. Perry Stone of Manna-Fest Ministries noted that some people have written that "the Scriptures are inaccurate because of the differing accounts about what happened to Judas". According to Stone, one needs only to go to Jerusalem to the spot where Judas hung himself, to clear up any confusion. Stone described what happened as follows: after the betrayal of Yeshua, Judas went to a tall hill to hang himself. He tied one end of a rope around his neck and tied the other end to a branch of a tree. As he jumped off the hill with a rope around his neck, the branch on which the other end of the rope hung broke, and he fell and tumbled down the steep slope. Acts 1:18-19 says: "Now this man acquired a field [called Hakeldama which means "Field of blood"] with the price of his wickedness, and falling headlong, he burst open in the middle and all his intestines gushed out".

Why Did Judas Betray Yeshua?

Judas was not saved. He had no personal relationship with Yeshua Jesus. This is why he could leave and betray the Lord so easily before the third cup of the

Passover meal was poured. He never called Yeshua Lord as the other disciples did. He always called Him rabbi. This means he simply thought of Yeshua as a teacher. He never professed faith in Him. He had expected Yeshua to overthrow the Roman Government and free the Jews from bondage, like what happened at the time of the battle of the Maccabees and is memorialized in the celebration of Chanukah. He did not realize that Yeshua came to earth the first time as the Lamb of God who would be cut off and hung on the cross for the sins of the world. In addition, Judas was consumed by greed. This is why he kept the money box. The disciples thought he did this to give money to the poor or buy what they needed, but that was not the case. He actually wanted it for himself. Judas died in the Potter's field that the Chief Priest and elders had purchased for a burial place for strangers with the blood money Judas had returned to them. This was predicted in the book of Jeremiah and recorded in Matthew 27:9.

Approximate Hours Following the Passover Seder that Lead up to Yeshua' Crucifixion – Copied by permission from Bible Study Fellowship International

In reading this timeline, it is important to remember that the Jews begin their new day at 6 p.m. in the evening. Thus their day runs from 6:00 p.m. one evening to 6:00 p.m. the following evening.

1:00 a.m. Prayer at Gethsemane
Judas' betrayal of Yeshua [Jesus] - [by a kiss]
Yeshua' arrest
The disciples desert Yeshua

2:00 a.m. Secret, first inquiry at Annas' house

3:00 a.m. Irregular trial at Caiaphas' house
Priests, teachers of the law and elders present
First mocking by the guards and others

5:00 a.m. Formal meeting of the Sanhedrin to confirm the death penalty

First Roman trial by Pilate
Examination by Herod
Second mocking by Herod and his men

6:30 a.m. Second Roman trial
Pilate's judgment [Crucifixion as the people requested]
The flogging [prerequisite to crucifixion by the Romans]
The third mocking by Roman soldiers

Crucifixion at the Place of the Skull:

9:00 a.m. Yeshua was being nailed to the cross, at the same time the lamb that was to be sacrificed was being tied on the altar in the temple.

12:00 Noon Darkness fell over all the land until 3:00 p.m.

3:00 p.m. Yeshua said, My God, My God, Why have You forsaken Me?' "It is finished" and He bowed His head and gave up His spirit.

Note: While Pastor Biltz was on tour in Jerusalem, his Orthodox Jewish tour guide taught that Yeshua was not put in a prison or a dungeon as many people believe. He was in a mikveh! He was allowed to go into a mikveh, an immersion pool, used by the High Priest. So Yeshua, our High Priest, was allowed to go up into a mikveh to purify [wash and cleanse] Himself before He became our sacrifice! It was there in the mikveh that he was placed under guard.

A mikveh was a small immersion pool that contained enough water to cover the entire body. It usually contained about 100-120 gallons when rainwater was its source however no distinction was made between fresh and salt water. Less water could be used if it was from a spring or fountain. All lakes and streams with flowing waters were acceptable for use as a mikveh except when used for waters of purification.

Many Christians blame the Jews for the death of Messiah Yeshua. Some blame both the Jews and the Romans. But the Bible says Yeshua gave up His own life. John 15:13 says: "Greater love has no one than this; that one lay down his life for his friends". But what was the role of the Jewish people? What was the role of the Romans? The Scripture has pointed out that the only ones ordained by God to offer sacrifices in the Temple were Aaron and his sons. Rabbi Cahn explained it this way: The sons of Aaron were "ordained by God to offer up the sacrifices. Why were they so obsessed with Messiah? They were the priests and He was the Lamb, the sacrifice. Only they could deliver the Lamb of God to His death. That's why they conspired and arrested Him and handed Him over to the Romans to be crucified". It was only through His crucifixion that the nation's sins could be forgiven. Messiah was the sacrificial lamb. As such, only the high priest who had to offer Him up as a sacrifice to God. The fact is the crucifixion of the son of God was determined before the foundation of the world, and both Jew and Gentile were ordained by the Father to play separate roles in the crucifixion of His Son, the Messiah. It was not an after thought by God. He was not caught off guard. He knew that only the blood of His Son could save and redeem mankind from the curse of sin.

The Death of Pontius Pilate

This decision to crucify Yeshua Jesus was a mistake in judgment on Pilate's part. He was a people-pleaser who was afraid to stand up to the Jews. It has been recorded that seven years after Yeshua Jesus was crucified, Pilate lost his job due to another error in judgment. He went out and hung himself just as Judas had done. He lost his career and his soul by seeking approval from the world.

The Scourging and Crucifixion of Yeshua Jesus

The following medical article was written by William D. Andrews, MD and published in the Journal of the American Medical Association, 1986.

Abstract

"Jesus of Nazareth underwent Jewish and Roman trials, was flogged, and was sentenced to death by crucifixion. The scourging produced deep stripe-like lacerations and appreciable blood loss, and it probably set the stage for hypovolemic shock, as evidenced by the fact that Jesus was too weakened to carry the crossbar (patibulum) to Golgotha. At the site of the crucifixion, His wrists were nailed to the patibulum and, after the patibulum was lifted onto the upright post (stipes), his feet were nailed to the stipes. The major pathophysiologic effect of crucifixion was an interference with normal respirations. Accordingly death resulted primarily from hypovolemic shock and exhaustion asphyxia. Jesus' death was ensured by the thrust of a soldier's spear into his side. Modern medical interpretation of the historical evidence indicates that Jesus was dead when taken down from the cross".

The most detailed description of the life and death of Yeshua is found in the four Gospel accounts; however, other writers also wrote about Him. Many references about Messiah can be found in the Talmud and in the book by Josephus, the Jewish historian of the first century. In the Talmud all rabbis agree that the Messiah would be a human being and a descendant of King David, and therefore, known as a son of David. Josephus questioned if Yeshua was even a man because of the miracles he performed; and the fact that many Jews and Gentiles came to faith in Him because of His teachings. After Pilate had condemned Him to death, even though he had found no fault in Him, over five hundred people reported having seen Yeshua Jesus after His death; that He was alive and arose from the grave after three days just as He had said. Many of the ancient prophets prophesized thousands of things the Messiah would do when He came to earth. Still many did not recognize or refused to believe in Him as their Lord while He was here on earth.

Dr. Chuck Missler has noted that "Yeshua's death was predicted by the angel Gabriel five centuries before He was nailed to that cross". On Nisan 13th [April 6th, 33 AD]. He had just completed the Passover meal with His disciples [all but Judas who had left before drinking the third cup; the "Cup of Redemption"], in the Upper Room and had walked with them to the Mount of Olives in the northeastern part of Jerusalem. Knowing His time of death was close at hand, Yeshua was emotionally suffering, and in agony. He knew the task that was laid before Him; that of taking upon Himself the sins of the whole world. He was in such a deep state of agony that He began to sweat great drops of blood [hemotidrosis]. As a result, His skin became very tender and fragile. After midnight, He was taken to the home of Annas and then to Caiaphas, the Jewish High Priest. He was later taken from there to the Temple and tried unfairly for blasphemy by Caiaphas and the Sanhedrin; a crime sentence that carried with it death. The guards blind folded Yeshua and hit Him with their fists. The High Priest took Him to the Roman Praetorium in the Antonia Fortress to get permission to have Him killed from Pontius Pilate. He said Yeshua was saying He was a king, not that He was guilty of blasphemy. Upon examination, Pilate found no wrong had been committed by Yeshua Jesus that was worthy of death. Pilate then passed Yeshua to Herod. Herod also found that Yeshua had committed no legal crime. Herod sent Yeshua back to Pilate. In an attempt to appease the people, Pilate decided to have Yeshua scourged. The instrument used was a short whip called a flagellum. It consisted of several strips of leather in which sharp pieces of bones or iron balls were embedded. When beaten by this instrument, a person's skin became a mass of quivering ribbons of blood and tissue. The loss of blood would produce a state of shock, and weaken the victim to the point of collapse or death. The beating given by one or two soldiers to Yeshua was particularly harsh and put Him in terrible pain. After the beating, He was mocked by the Roman soldiers. A crown made from 6 inch long sharp thorns [from either the thorn bush or Euphorbia milii] was pushed into the skin on His forehead. A purple robe of a king was placed on His shoulders and a wooden staff was put in His right hand as a scepter. In this weakened state, Yeshua was then forced to carry a patibulum [crossbar] up the hill to Golgotha, the Place of the Skull, where He was hung between two thieves. Due to the awful beating, no water, no food, cold, and no sleep, Yeshua died, according to Dr. Andrews, of hypovolemic shock and exhaustion asphyxia before the Roman Soldier thrust his spear into Yeshua' side. On His cross Pilate had written the words, "YESHUA OF NAZARENE AND THE KING OF THE JEWS". The chief priests of the Jews asked Pilate not to write those words but Pilate said, "What I have written I have written" – John 19:22. Why was the chief priest so upset about what Pilate wrote? Because in Hebrew, the beginning letters of what was written spelled out YHWH, the tetragrammaton for the name of God. The Jews didn't want to acknowledge that it was their Messiah who was hanging on that cross.

Order Followed in Passover Today

During the days before the Passover feast anything containing leaven/ yeast is removed from the house. Leaven represents sin. It is where the idea of Spring cleaning comes from! The implements used are: a candle, a feather, a wooden spoon, and a white cloth. Pastor Biltz explains the procedure this way: "the father carries the candle. It represents the light of God's word that reveals sin. The child carries the feather which is the Holy Spirit. When he finds the hidden leaven, he points at it with the feather but is told not to touch it. The father then uses the feather to sweep the leaven into the wooden spoon. The wooden spoon represents the cross of Yeshua. The leaven is then wrapped in the white cloth, just as Yeshua was when laid in the tomb wrapped in a white burial cloth. The cloth is then taken outside the house to a place where it is burned. Like Yeshua, it represents a sacrificial offering on our behalf. Yeshua also helped His Father get the leaven out of His house when He turned over the tables of the moneychangers and sellers in the Temple".

The Procedure for the Passover Seder Meal

The order for Passover presented in this book was summarized from "The Messianic Passover Haggadah", a booklet that gives the order in which the Seder meal is to be conducted by Barry and Steffi Rubin and The Passover Seder for Believers in Yeshua by El Shaddai Ministries. The word Haggadah means "the telling" in Hebrew. Passover is the miraculous story of how God freed the Jews from Egyptian slavery. It has been recounted yearly as a memorial of the event. It tells the timeless truth of how God loves and cares for the children of Israel.

During the time of Yeshua Jesus, the invited quests and family members were invited to recline at the table. This was the action of a free man, not a slave, as slaves had to stand. To begin the Passover meal, the woman of the house lights the candles and prays for illumination to God in whose name she lights the festival lights. The host then washes his hands. This demonstrated his importance at the table and sets him apart from the others who are in attendance. It is important to note that Yeshua did not set Himself up as more important than those at His table. Instead He chose to wash His disciples' feet as a sign of humility.

The host then recited the Kiddush, the prayer of sanctification. Afterwards he pours the first cup of wine. The wine used must be a red wine [or grape juice] that was mixed with warm water. For a Christian, we instantly see the connection between the red wine mixed with water and the image of Yeshua Jesus hanging dead on the cross, with blood and water pouring out from His wounded side where the Roman soldier had taken his spear and thrust it into Yeshua Jesus' side to prove He was dead. The hand washing is also a reminder that Yeshua washed us clean with His blood and has given us the Holy Spirit as living water.

Next, a bitter herb such as lettuce, parsley was dipped into a small basin of salt water or vinegar and passed around the table for all to eat. It represented the tears shed in Egypt. After partaking of the bitter herb, a second cup of wine was poured, but not drank at this point. A young child then asks the Four Questions concerning how this night is different from other nights. The host answers the questions the child had asked. He explains the meaning of the matzah, the bitter herbs, the lamb, and why the Jewish people ate in a reclined position on this night.

The host then tells the history of the Jewish people and their first Passover. Food symbolic items on the Seder plate are brought in and the host explains the meaning of each item on the plate. The host and guests then recount the ten plagues of Egypt. As the name of each plague is mentioned one dips their small finger into the wine, "allowing a drop of liquid to fall, reducing the fullness of our cup of joy this night".

The host washes his hands a second time. He then broke a piece of the matzah and gives a prayer of thanksgiving over the bread. The host then dips the matzah in salt water which represents tears. He adds a small amount of a sweet mixture of apples, nuts, and honey on top of matzah. The matzah is shared.

After this, the meal is eaten. The Jews do not serve lamb since they no longer have their Temple in Jerusalem, so chicken or beef are used as a substitute for the lamb.

After supper, the third cup of wine, the Cup of Redemption, is poured, and thanks are given to God. After the wine is consumed, Psalms 115-118, known as the Hallel, is recited.

A fourth cup of wine, called by some as the cup of Elijah is then poured and drank. The Seder meal ends with the song, Dayenu, which means "It would have been enough for us", or a hymn. The meal to complete with everyone saying, "Next Year in Jerusalem"!

This expression represents the liberation and redemption of the Jewish people as they dream of making aliyah to their ancient homeland, Jerusalem, Israel.

6 Common Questions People Ask About Passover by Pastor Mark Biltz

"Why was the lamb roasted? Yeshua was the burnt offering sacrifice".

"Why not boiled in water? There is no watering down the word of God".

"Why unleavened bread? Yeshua was without sin".

"Why eaten with bitter herbs? Because of the bitterness Yeshua went through".

"Why the following morning burned with fire? Yeshua Jesus was our burnt offering".

He would be sacrificed on Passover whole, without a single bone being broken. "Why do they recline at a Seder? Because they were free men, not slaves". Slaves were required to stand up while eating their meal.

Types of Animal Sacrifices That Were Performed by The Jewish People

There were two types of offerings – voluntary and mandatory. The voluntary offering allowed us to demonstrate our love for God. The mandatory offering were for forgiveness of unintentional sins which are sins done in ignorance. The sacrificial system had nothing to do with intentional sins since intentional sins were not atoned for through offerings but through other forms of restitution. All of the laws concerning sacrifices were assigned by rabbinic tradition since the Torah was silent on the subject.

Note: On Passover, April 2017, an animal sacrifice was performed near the Temple Mount in Jerusalem for the first time in over 2,000 years. Over two hundred people participated in this ceremony!

Types of Offerings:

1. The Burnt offering, also called the Olah offering, meaning "to rise or ascend". It was first in a level of sacredness. It was a voluntary offering that was totally consumed by fire and dedicated to God. No one was allowed to eat from it. It represented complete surrender to God. Whole animals were cut into pieces and their blood was poured out on the sides of the altar. Small birds such as turtledoves or young pigeons were not cut up and their blood was poured out on the side of the altar. Size of the offering didn't matter to God. All He wants is the right attitude. Anyone could give something to God, regardless of their statue. He saw an animal's life's as sacred, the same way He sees a human's life, and the blood was a substitute for sin. Read: Leviticus 1:1-17, 6:8-13.
2. The Grain offering was an offering of fine flour mixed with oil and frankincense. It was prepared on a pan or griddle and formed into cakes and wafers. A handful was burnt on the altar for God and the rest was given the sons of Aaron, the priests. This offering pointed to our Messiah, the bread of life. Read: Leviticus 2:1-16, Leviticus 2:5-7, and Leviticus 6:14-23.
3. The Peace offering was a voluntary offering. It was shared with the priests, with God, and by the person who offered it. It represented the Passover meal and was a way for the Hebrew people to show God their love for Him. Our Messiah who was the peace offering for those of us who believe in Him. Read: Leviticus 3:1-17, 7:11-36.
4. The Sin offering was a mandatory offering of sacredness second only to that of the burnt offering. It was given by an individual who had committed an unintentional sin through carelessness, not an intentional sin. It was meant to restore fellowship with God. Read: Leviticus 4:1-5, 6:24-7:7.
5. The Guilt/Trespass offering was also known as the ***Asham*** offering. It was restitution for damages done to someone else that required

a monetary payment to them. Its level of sacredness was third in order of the sacrifices. Read: Leviticus 5:14, 6:7, 7:1-7. Rabbi Jonathan Cahn in his book, "The Book of Mysteries" said that "the guilt offering could only take away the guilt of the one offering it by first becoming the guilt". That is what Yeshua Jesus did. He became our guilt and our sin on that old wooden cross so we could be redeemed. Rabbi Cahn further noted that guilt and sin is called ***Asham*** in Hebrew; and therefore "if Messiah is the Asham and the Asham is the guilt, then if the Asham dies, so too has died all your guilt, all your shame, and all your regrets. They've all died and are gone...completely and forever...It is finished".

6. The "Pesah or Paschal sacrifice" was different from the other offerings in that the laws that had to be followed were different. To the Christian, the offering of the Paschal lamb is particularly significant. It represents Yeshua Jesus who fulfilled the sacrifices for the sins of the world which enabled us to be redeemed and considered to be a child of God.

"The name Elohim always refers to judgment, so it was never used in connection with the offerings or sacrifices" according to Pastor Biltz. Only the name LORD was used because it represented mercy, the YHWH [the tetragrammaton of the name of God]. The Jewish people prefer to use the YHWH since the name of God was/is considered too holy to speak out loud. The offerings and sacrifices were meant to draw them closer to a merciful God. They did not serve as an appeasement to a harsh and false god as was done in the pagan system. Thus the sacrifices by the Jews were to the true God and were accompanied by wine and water libations. The first three were voluntary freewill offerings that were used to enhance their relationship with God. The last two were mandatory offerings used to rectify sin and mend their relationship with God. The mandatory sacrifices required the individual to acknowledge their responsibility for their transgressions, repent, and make restitution if required.

Can We Ever Repay God for Sending Yeshua Jesus?

Yeshua Jesus fulfilled all the offerings. "He paid the debt we could never pay" – Biltz. He changed our intentional sins to unintentional sins so we could be saved. He is the Paschal sacrifice. He is our burnt offering, our grain offering, our peace offering, our sin offering, and our guilt offering. The only way we can repay God is to accept His Son, Yeshua Jesus, as our Messiah, King, Lord, and Savior. Our primary purpose is to glorify the Lord Yeshua, bring others, both Jew and Gentile, into the saving knowledge of Him, and take physical and emotional care of the children of Israel.

Why will the sacrificial system return during the Millennial Reign since Yeshua fulfilled the need for an offering?

God placed the desire to worship Him in the heart of man. Therefore mankind can not restrain himself from worshipping. In the ancient past, people drew pictures on the walls of their homes, in caves and carved idols of stone and wood as objects for worship. This was man's attempt to visualize what God looked like. We immediately think of the Golden Calf when we think of idol worship or how Terah, Abram's father, was an idol maker for Nimrod. As time went on, however, man convinced himself that he did not need to worship the Creator God or engage in idol worship. Instead he relied on his own intellect as the way to make himself higher than the heavens. Still it was difficult not to seek something higher than oneself in order to survive. As the familiar saying goes, there are no atheists in fox holes. The counter-balance to idolatry was the sacrificial system. It will be used in the Third Temple during the Millennial Reign of Yeshua Jesus as a way to honor and commemorate what He, the Lamb of God, did on the cross for those who believe in Him.

To enter into heaven a person must accept Yeshua Jesus as their personal Lord and Savior. The Lord separates believers from non-believers like the wheat from the tares and is coming back only for His own. Many people blaspheme the Lord both now and in the future. They will not repent or ask for forgiveness and will therefore not be saved from eternal damnation and total separation from the Creator. Some people will brag about their sins and curse God. They will take the mark of the Beast. It is scary to contemplate, but some people believe that once the mark of the beast is taken, a person's DNA is permanently altered so they will never again have the chance to be redeemed. Others believe that the mark of the beast will change one's internal frequency; the frequency that is left over from God's voice in Creation. Many of the Jews during the Tribulation will refuse the mark. They will recognize and surrender to Yeshua as their Messiah, even if it cost them their lives. When they die for their faith in Yeshua, their defilement will be cleansed by the blood of the Lamb, and they will be redeemed.

Petra, Jordan

Petra is located in what was once considered northern Arabia but is now in the country of Jordan. The city is located 140 miles south of Amman, the capital of Jordan, and 120 miles southeast of Jerusalem. It is an ancient city that was carved out of sandstone rock cliffs from the top down. The beautiful colors of tan, yellow, pink and burgundy of the stones are caused by iron and silica particles that flow through the rocks from underground springs. Ken Klein, of Ken Klein Productions, recorded that Petra is considered "the most mysterious ghost town in the world". It has, however, over one million visitors yearly from all over the world.

Petra has been called by several names in the Scriptures. The most common are: Selah, Mount Horeb, and Mount Seir. It was rediscovered in 1812 by John Burkhart, a Swiss explorer, after having been lost over a millennium. God will protect a remnant of Jews there during the second half of the Tribulation Period. Messiah Jesus and His redeemed saints will come to Bozrah, "the gateway to Petra", during the last battle of Armageddon and defeat the nations and people who have fought against and attempted to destroy Israel.

Many groups of people have lived in the caves in Petra until fairly recently. The government of Jordan, realizing the value of Petra as a tourist site, had the residents of the area move into homes they built for them in the modern city of Petra. Some of Petra's historical residents included the Edomites who were descendants of Esau, the Nabateans who were descendants of Ishmael and in more modern times, the Bedouins. When Esau and Jacob parted ways, after Jacob exchanged Esau's birthright for a pot of soup – Genesis 27, Jacob fled north and Esau went south. Esau's city known as Petra is hidden in a deep crevice thought to be caused by an ancient volcano. It is surrounded by rugged sandstone mountains. By the time of the Romans, Petra became a well known trading center with a population of approximately one million people. It housed a Roman amphitheater which speaks of its importance. Many remnants of the Roman period are still visible, most particularly the Roman road leading from the entrance to the city. The city entrance is called the Siq. It is an opening between two boulders. Once through the Siq, one travels downward to the ancient city of Petra which is located just over a mile in distance. In places the road is so narrow that it is said to be no wider than the width of one Roman chariot. This made the city very defendable from attacks by its enemies.

Note: During the Tribulation period, a remnant consisting of 1/4 of the Jews will flee from Jerusalem to the rugged mountains of Petra, Jordan. There they will live in the caves in the area and be protected and keep safe by God.

In the DVD by Klein titled "Petra: Israel's Secret Hiding Place" it is recorded that Petra has been visited by many people spoken of in the Scriptures and in history. Some cited were: Abraham, Job, Moses, Aaron, and David when he was running from King Saul and killed 18,000 Edomites – II Samuel 8. Antony and Cleopatra, King Herod, who was the Edomite who tried to destroy all baby body under the age of two, Alexander the Great, when he was on his way to India, and Lawrence of Arabia, of World War II fame, all visited Petra. Aaron's tomb is located on a mountaintop on the way to Petra from the modern resort city of Aqaba, Jordan.

My Personal Journey to Petra

In March, 2011 my husband and I had the blessed opportunity to travel to Israel and Jordan. Both countries were amazing and many things stand out in my mind about the trip. We left the City of Eilat, Israel for Aqaba,

Jordan on a warm, sunny day. After a short drive we came to the border. There we were informed that we had to walk the 50 yards or so from Israel into Jordan. Once we arrived into Jordan, we waited in Customs for a couple hours while they checked our passports and credentials. Finally we were given permission to aboard a Jordanian bus to continue our journey. We arrived at Aqaba, Jordan in the afternoon and checked into a Days Inn Hotel. In the center was a large courtyard from which one could look up 5-6 stories. Most notable were the strings of green plants hanging from the short glass walls that faced the courtyard. After unpacking our belongings, we joined up with other people from our tour group and set out to explore the city. Aqaba was a modern city built within walking distance of the Sea of Aqaba [Red Sea]. Surrounding it was a mountainous, barren wilderness. Everything was beige in color and there were few trees to be seen anywhere. Close by the hotel was a tall, narrow tower from which the call of prayer was sounded. We went into an ice cream parlor and treated ourselves to a delicious ice cream cone. After touring the city we returned to our hotel for the night. About 4:30 a.m. we were awakened by the Muslim call for prayer. We could see the tower of the mosque from our window, and to our surprise we could also see several American fast food restaurants. After being awakened, we quickly dressed, ate breakfast, boarded our tour bus, and headed for Petra. On the way there we saw Aaron's Tomb shining white in the sun and sitting high on a mountaintop. After a short drive, we reached the modern city of Petra. It consisted of small beige homes sitting on the hills. After another short drive we arrived at the ancient city of Petra. After the bus parked, we gathered together and walked down a wide, long, dirt road. On the each side of the road were sandstone caves; many with narrow stairways caved into the rocks. After the short walk we arrived at the front of the Siq where there were small shops which contained items for tourists and drinking water. Children ran around the area hawking jewelry, maps, postcards, and other small items. Guards dressed in costume like Nabateans stood at the entrance of the Siq. As one entered the Siq, the passage way narrowed. At times it was only wide enough for a single chariot. Periodically tourists on horses or in small, horse drawn carts passed us on the road. Tall rose-colored and tan rocks rose high into the blue sky. At times, the roof of the passageway was almost covered over by large stones 40 or more feet high. This created beautiful shadows on the old Roman stone road we were walking on as we walked downhill toward the city. We passed a water system carved out of the rock during the first century and saw several stone carvings of idols. Suddenly, we arrived at a narrow opening through which we could see a tall, beautifully carved building known as the Treasury across the courtyard! This building was carved from the top down and stood over 100 feet tall. It had huge columns on each side of the door, with men dressed as Nabateans standing by. As we stepped out of the Siq, we entered into a large, dusty courtyard that contained several make shift shops. There were musicians playing unknown instruments sitting against the rock walls. Camels were there for tourists to ride as well as horses to rent and buggies for hire. To the left, were many small, caves. We were told these were the homes of poor families at one time. Down and to the right were tall, beautifully carved caves and tombs. We went into one of the caves and felt the cool temperature inside. It was dark with only the door as a source of light. Beyond those caves was a Roman Amphitheater and other ancient carvings to see. By the end of the day, we were exhausted and still had the mile-long hill to climb through the Siq to get back to our bus. My husband and I chose to ride a horse back up. The only problem was they did not have a saddle horn to grab hold of when attempting to get in the saddle. Seeing my problem, one of the guides of grabbed my opposite leg and pulled me across and onto the horses' back. He led me gently up the hill. The next problem, of course, was getting off. Again, the guide used his ingenuity and pushed my leg over the saddle and onto the ground. What an experience!

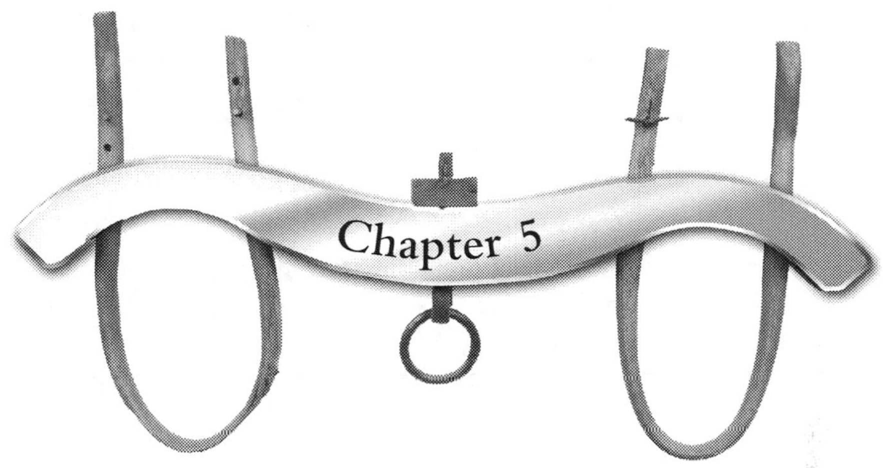

Chapter 5

The Feast of Unleavened Bread

The Feast of Unleavened Bread is the second Spring feast that was fulfilled by Yeshua at the time of His first coming. It begins on Nisan 15, the day after Passover. The Jews consider Unleavened Bread an extension of Passover. They have faithfully kept this feast for over fifteen hundred generations!

To the Jews: the week of this feast is a memorial marking their freedom from Egyptian bondage.

To the Christians: Yeshua Jesus is the unleavened bread since He is without sin. It is also the time when Yeshua was in the tomb for three days after His resurrection.

For the Jew, unleavened bread is called "the bread of affliction". It is a reminder of their having to flee Egypt so quickly that there wasn't time for the yeast to rise in the dough. They call this special bread that contained no yeast, matzah. Ceil and Moishe Rosen said of matzah, "It typified the sweetness and wholesomeness of life without sin". It looks like a light beige-colored cracker that has been striped, pierced and bruised by fire. Leviticus 23:6 says: "Then on the fifteenth day of the same month [Nisan] there is a Feast of Unleavened Bread to the Lord; for seven days you shall eat unleavened bread".

For the Christian, matzah represents the sinless body of Yeshua, who was pierced, striped, and beaten by the Roman soldier's whip. He is the bread of life sent down from heaven to redeem sinful humanity who believed in Him. Dr. Booker described the Lord's sacrifice in another descriptive and poignant way. He said, "Jesus took our leaven of sin in His spirit, our leaven of sorrows in His soul, and our leaven of sickness, disease, and death in His body".

Michael Norten wrote that the Feast of Unleavened Bread "teaches the concept of our being in fellowship with the Lord". In the book of Genesis we learn that God comes and walks in the garden with Adam and Eve in the cool of the day, before their fall. It is easy to see that both God and His creation were in harmony and enjoyed fellowship with each other. The problem came when Adam and Eve decided to believe the lie of the serpent rather than to trust and believe in God's word. They ate of the tree of knowledge of good and evil and their eyes were opened. They then hid from God in their shame when He came to fellowship with them in the evening. How incredibly sad! They had everything in the garden but that one tree; the tree that belonged to God, and they wanted that one too! They wanted to be in charge not God. After the fall, their connection with God was spiritually broken. How sad God must have felt knowing the choice they made. Still in His love, He clothed them with animal skins rather than leaving them in the leaves they had used to cover their bodies with and send them out east of the garden. He then stationed His cherubim at the door of the Garden of Eden with a flaming sword to keep Adam and Eve from returning. Why? Was God being cruel? No, God was not being cruel, but loving. He did not want them to eat of the tree of life again and die without a hope of redemption. Dr. Richard Booker wrote that "the Feast of Unleavened Bread represents the work of God's Holy Spirit which enables us to live a holy life". This transforming work in man's heart is called "sanctification". This is what creates true faith and not a faith based on the work of one's hands. The cleansing work of the Holy Spirit extends all the way to our thoughts, words, and deeds.

How Yeshua Fulfilled the Feast of Unleavened Bread

Dr. Chuck Missler explains that Yeshua was taken off the cross and carried to the tomb by Joseph of Arimathea, a member of the Sanhedrin and "a wealthy kinsman of Yeshua". The Apostle Luke described Joseph as "a good and righteous man, from a city of the Jews, who was waiting for the kingdom of God" – Luke 23:50-53. Joseph had not agreed with the plan of the High Priest and Pharisees to crucify the Lord for he was a secret disciple of Yeshua but he had a fear of the Jews. However, once Yeshua Jesus was crucified, he went to Pilate and asked for Yeshua's body. Having been given permission, he took the body, and with the help of Nicodemus wrapped it in a linen cloth, and laid it in his own tomb, where no one had ever laid. John 19:39 adds that Nicodemus brought a hundred pounds of an embalming/anointing mixture consisting of an aromatic gum called myrrh and a fragrant wood known as aloes that was pounded into powder, to be used to anoint the body of Messiah. Dr. Booker noted that there are two thoughts about the amount of anointing mixture used on a body of a deceased person. First, he said, many believe "the amount of spices used to anoint the body was a measure of the value of the deceased or second, perhaps half the weight of a person's body". For example, the Jews greatly esteemed Rabbi Gamaliel so they wrapped him with eighty pounds of spices after his death. In the case of Yeshua Jesus, His disciples used a mixture of a hundred pounds of myrrh and aloes [spices] to bind the linen wrapping around His body when He was in the grave. This would indicate that Yeshua Jesus was more highly esteemed than Rabbi Gamaliel was by His followers! If one uses one's weight to determine their value, Yeshua Jesus would have outweighed Rabbi Gamaliel by forty pounds.

The body of the deceased was prepared for burial in the following manner. The spices used [aloe and myrrh] where mixed together to form a paste. This paste was put on the linen strips. These strips were then wrapped around the body of the deceased from the shoulder down to the toe. Once dried, they formed a stiff cocoon-like covering over the body. A linen burial cloth was then laid over the face of the deceased.

The Scriptures tell us that the body of Yeshua was hurriedly prepared and His tomb was sealed. Roman guards were ordered to stand on each side of the large stone that was placed over the opening of the tomb. This request was made by the High Priest to Pilate to make sure that no one stole the body. The tomb was secured by stretching a cord across the stone and sealed at each end with a Roman seal. This was to remain in place for three days.

After the Sabbath, on the first day of the week, Mary Magdalene, Mary the mother of James and Joseph, Salome, and Johanna came to anoint the body with the spices, but an earthquake had occurred and the tomb was empty expect for an angel. The angel said to the women, "Do not be afraid; for I know that you are looking for Jesus who has been crucified. He is not here, for He has risen, just as He said. Come, see the place where He was lying"- Matthew 28:6. And they left the tomb quickly with fear and great joy and ran to report it to His disciples. And behold, Jesus met them and greeted them. And they came up and took hold of His feet and worshiped Him.

The Great Lie

Why were the soldiers afraid? It was not only because they experience an earthquake, saw the angel at the tomb, though those two things would probably frighten anyone, but most of all they knew they would be killed if they had left their post or had fallen asleep while on duty. Still, the tomb was obviously empty that they had been instructed to guard. What were they to do? Would anyone believe them if they told them what really happened? They were in a no-win situation. The Bible tells us that a huge earthquake had occurred at the time the stone was removed by an angel of the Lord. "His appearance was like lightning, and his clothing as white as snow. The guards shook for fear of him and became like dead men" – Matthew 28:3-4. The soldiers decided to inform to the High Priest. After the Chief Priest was told what had happened, he gave the soldiers a large sum of money and told to say, 'His disciples came by night and stole Him away while we were asleep'. The Chief Priest told the soldiers he would keep them out of trouble if they did want they were told. The soldiers took the money and did as they were instructed. Their lie was spread among the Jews and has been believed by them until this day. The truth is Yeshua Jesus, the Messiah, rose from the dead on the third day and by so doing fulfilled the Feast of Unleavened Bread.

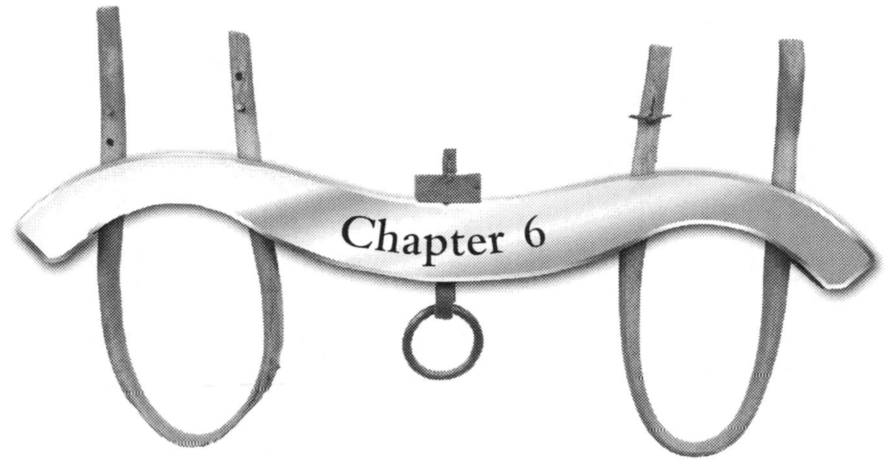

The Feast of Firstfruits

First Fruits is a major celebration following Unleavened Bread. This celebration is the third Spring feast that Yeshua fulfilled during His First Coming. It is the only feast that has the Resurrection of Yeshua Jesus as its focal point. The Gospel accounts tell us that on the first day of this feast [Nisan 18] Yeshua was resurrected from the dead, and became the First Fruit of those who had fallen asleep [had died]. Born-again believers in Yeshua as Lord and Savior call this day "Easter" or "Resurrection Day". Some people prefer to use the name Resurrection Day rather than Easter because "they believe that the name 'Easter' is derived from various pagan goddesses of fertility, according to Dr. Todd Baker of The Levitt Letter, such as Ishtar (Babylonian-Assyrian), Astarte (Phoenician), or Eostre/Eastre (Teutonic). According Baker, the name Easter actually may be of Saxon origin and the equivalent of the German "Ostern" which means: "east", "dawn", "new light", and by extension 'resurrection'".

To the ancient Jewish people, the Feast of First Fruits denoted the annual harvest in which the first fruits of one's labors were presented to the priest. Exodus 23:16 says, "Also you shall observe the Feast of the Harvest of the first fruits of your labors from what you sow in the field; also the Feast of the Ingathering at the end of the year when you gather in the fruit of your labors from the field."

To the Jews: The sheaf that is placed before the Lord and blessed by the priest resulted in the entire harvest being blessed by the Lord. The baked loaves were a wave offering to the Lord.

To the Christians: Messiah Yeshua became the first fruit of all creation when He arose on the first day of First Fruits and offered Himself to His Father as the first fruits from the dead. This fact was recorded in all four Gospel accounts which tell us that the women went to the tomb on the first day of the week after the Passover and found it empty. Christians believe that the two loaves of leavened bread that are waved before the Lord represent the Jew and the Gentle, both of whom have come together united in their belief of Yeshua Jesus as Messiah and Lord!

Bringing in the Firstfruits

During the time of the Temple when a man went out into his field and saw ripe figs, ripe grapes or a ripe pomegranate, he would tie reed grass around the ripened fruit to designate it as firstfruits. Firstfruits were not limited to fruits alone, however. They included the seven species that were praised in the Torah as the finest produce in Israel. They included not only figs, grapes and pomegranates, but also wheat, barley, olives, and dates for honey – Deuteronomy 8:8.

The pageantry of the Feast of First Fruits celebration has been characterized as follows: After the first fruits had ripened, whole families and others from the same community would go together to the Temple. Large groups of pilgrims would travel together because it was too dangerous to travel alone. They would walk by foot with their baskets full of fruits and grains. Those who lived close to Jerusalem brought fresh figs, grapes and grains while those who lived further away brought dried fruits and other produce. The produce was restricted to the seven types that grew in Israel: wheat, barley, grapes, figs, pomegranates, olives and dates. Turtledoves were tied to each basket that would be offered up as a burnt offering to the Lord. People of wealth had fruit filled baskets that were overlaid with silver and gold. The people of lesser means brought their produce in wicker baskets made of peeled willow branches. Regardless of the type of basket, the filled baskets were presented to the priests at the Temple so the remaining crops would be blessed by the Lord.

An ox with its horns covered in gold led the procession just behind the flute player. It had an olive-wreath on its head. A flute was played in front of the procession, to maintain the tempo, until just before their arrived at the Temple Mount in Jerusalem. As the people came close to Jerusalem, they sent out messengers to announce their arrival as they ornamentally arranged their produce. Everyone of importance came out of the temple to meet the pilgrims with shouts of joy and playing flutes. The number of officials meeting the pilgrims varied in number according to the rank of the pilgrims. The greeting officials included governors of priest, chiefs of the Levites, and treasurers of the temple. All the artisans of Jerusalem would rise before them and greet them with "Our brothers, men of [name of their town], enter in peace". When the pilgrims reached the Temple Mount, each man with baskets still on his shoulders, would recite Deuteronomy 26:3-10. The baskets were then deposited by the side of the altar, as each man prostrated himself, thanked God for all things, both good and bad and then departed. Even King Agrippa would take a basket, place it on his shoulders, and walk as far as the Temple Court. When they reached the Court, the Levites would sing Psalm 30:2 which said, "I will extol Thee, O Lord, for Thou has raised me up, and has not suffered my enemies to rejoice over me". This obeisance showed their thankfulness for the entire process of their history, from the Exodus to their farming the land, and to bringing of the firstfruits in the land of Israel to God. The ox was sacrificed as a peace offering to God. As God accepted their sacrifice, He showed that He had fulfilled His promise to honor them above all nations because they kept His commandments.

The first fruits of the harvest are called the *bikoreem* in Hebrew. This means to "shoot out or to burst open". This is what Yeshua Jesus did! He burst out from the confines of the grave and rose, with others who had come out of their graves, into heaven and presented Himself and the gift of His firstfruits to the Father! God said the first fruit of the womb and of the flocks are holy and belong to Him – Exodus 13:1-2. They are the most anointed. Yeshua Jesus, the anointed one, became the first fruit of heaven after He arose. This is why He did not want Mary to cling to Him just after He rose out of the grave. His death on the cross tore open the veil in the Holy of Holies that had separated believers from God. Now we can all freely go to Him.

Leviticus 23:9-11 says: "Then the Lord spoke to Moses, saying, "Speak to the sons of Israel and say to them, 'When you enter the land which I am going to give to you and reap its harvest, then you shall bring in the sheaf of the first fruits of your harvest to the priest. He shall wave the sheaf before the Lord for you to be accepted; on the day after the Sabbath the priest shall wave it".

These verses point out two things: 1) the Jews will be in the land of Israel when they celebrate this feast, and 2) First Fruits will be observed during the time of the barley harvest.

The period of time between First Fruits and Shavuot /Pentecost is fifty days. These fifty days are known as "the counting of the Omer". The first grain to mature in Israel is barley. A half-gallon of barley was called an Omer. Dr. Booker outlines the process used by the ancient Jews during this feast and Michael Norten adds to the description. "The first barley to mature was marked by a red cord and bound into a sheaf". The marked sheaves were cut in the afternoon, just before sunset. They were then taken to the Court of the Temple where they were thrashed out with canes, then parched on a pan perforated with holes, so each grain might be touched by the fire. The Omer was mixed with three-fourths of a pint of oil, and a handful of frankincense. It is then waved before the Lord, and a handful was taken out and burned on the altar". This procedure makes all the barley in the field kosher and holy by consecrating the harvest to God. It also shows that the farmer had total dependence on God.

Sam Nadler speaks of first fruits and second fruits. As we know, the First Fruits offering were of barley. Barley was considered God's provision for a poor man. It also represented believers in Messiah made in the image of His body. The second offering was of wheat. It was considered a rich man's food. The final first fruit believers will be Jews who have accepted Yeshua during the Tribulation Period and the 144,000 Jews "having His name and the name of His Father written on their foreheads" – Revelation 14:1. The 144,000 were made up of every Jewish tribe except the tribe of Dan. The Tribe of Dan represents the Gentiles. The believing Gentiles will be absent from the Tribulation because they were taken up to heaven in the Rapture. The believing Jews from the Tribulation Period are part of the wheat harvest.

The Harvest and the Resurrection

The order of harvests corresponds with the resurrection of believers. The first crop to mature in the early Spring in Israel is barley. It is a soft grain that is willowed. In the field it looks like its head is bowed down in prayer and humility. It is the first grain to be harvested. The believing church is the first to be resurrected at the end of the age when believers are given their spiritual bodies in the Rapture. Most born-again believers hold that the timing of the Rapture is prior to the Tribulation Period; some however believe the Rapture will occur in the middle of the Tribulation, and still other believe that it will happen at the end. Regardless of the timing, born-again believers are the first fruits of Zion.

In the late Spring in Israel the wheat harvest begins. The head of the wheat is hard and stands up so it must be crushed on a tribulum to separate the wheat from the chaff. The tribulum is a large board with bits of glass or stones attached underneath it. As a horse pulls the tribulum over the wheat, the wheat is crushed. This is symbolic of the Jews who will be crushed under the tribulum and harvested during the Tribulation Period. The 144,000 Jewish evangelists during the Tribulation Period are considered the first fruits of the wheat.

In the beginning of the Fall harvest, grapes are picked and placed in winepresses to make wine. This time of year connects with the Battle of Armageddon at the end of the Tribulation Period and Messiah's Second Coming which will put an end to the battle. Unbelievers will be taken away to the White Throne Judgment at the end of the Millennial Reign of Yeshua Jesus and cast into the lake of fire in outer darkness.

The last of the harvest is the gleanings. These are not harvested and represent those believers who survived the Tribulation Period and entered the Millennial Reign of Yeshua Jesus in their mortal bodies – Matthew 24:31.

A Personal Easter Experience

I will never forget the Easter weekend services that were held at Mariners Church in Irvine, California. Even though it has been over twenty years since I was there, it feels like it was yesterday. It celebration began on Friday before Resurrection Sunday. On Good Friday as we entered into the darkened sanctuary each person was given a small piece of flash paper and a pencil. We were instructed to write down our sins on the paper. Large wooden crosses had been placed in various areas around the sanctuary – several in the front, several at each of the sides and several toward the back. All the windows of the sanctuary were covered in black. No songs were sung. At the end of a very quiet, poignant service in which the words and emotions of Yeshua were printed one by one on a large screen, each person walked alone to one of the wooden crosses. There they were handed a hammer and a nail with which to nail their sin covered paper on the cross. Afterwards, each person participated in Communion and returned to their seat. All one could hear in that huge, darkened church was the sound of a hammer nailing each person's sins on the cross. It was like being a participant at the crucifixion of Yeshua, and putting all our guilt and sin on Him so we could be cleansed and saved. It brought home the fact that the sins we engage in are most often physical actions of choice, but the resulting guilt is an emotional response we carry as a result of the action we chose to engage in. One is never free of their guilt or sins until they have surrendered all to Yeshua and accepted Him as their Lord and Savior. On Sunday, when we walked into the church all the lights were on and the window coverings had been removed. It was light and bright. The songs we sang were upbeat and joyful. He has Risen – Hallelujah!! The light of God has overcome the darkness in this world!

How the Feast of Firstfruits is Celebrated in Israel Today

In Israel today, Jewish adults leave mounds of fruit in the courtyard of the Jewish Agency building for distribution to the poor or for sale. The children participate in a parade and carry various agricultural products to be given to the Jewish National Fund for land reclamation.

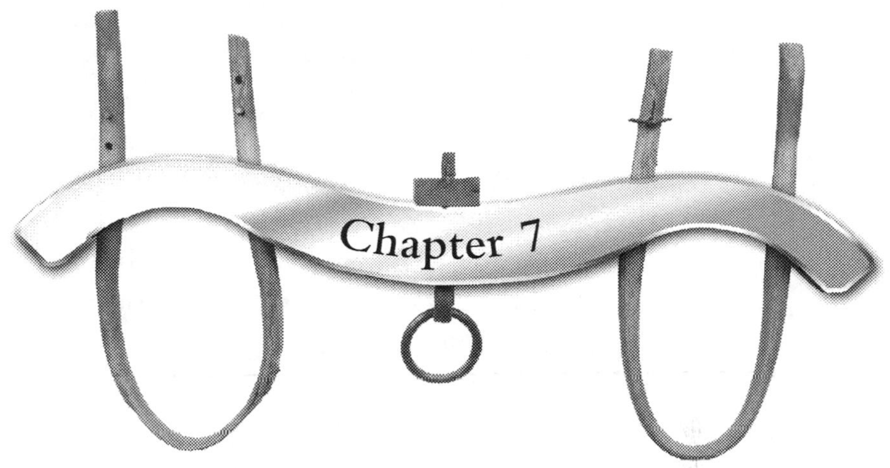

The Feast of Pentecost/The Feast of Weeks/Shavuot

The word Pentecost which means "fifty" is one of the three pilgrimage feasts that are required to be observed in Jerusalem by God's covenant people. It occurs fifty days after First Fruits but no specific date was designated by the Lord. This is unusual since all other feasts were given specific dates on which to be observed. This is why some Christian theologians and Bible experts, like Dr. Chuck Missler, believe the Rapture of the church will occur at this time. The church, like Moses, will be born and die on the same day.

The Jews call the seven weeks that lead up to Pentecost from Passover, the Feast of Weeks or Shavuot. This is when they were "counting the Omer" and waiting for the time when all the barley would be mature and ready to harvest. These fifty days end at the Feast of Shavuot. "In the festival, they [the Jews] commemorate the symbolism of the marriage between God, the Groom, and Israel His bride", according to Gary Stearman in his article titled: "Pentecost 2017: Reviewing the Rapture". Shavuot also commemorates the giving of the Torah to Moses by God.

Shavuot is represented by two loaves of leavened bread which were prepared from the first harvest. The two loaves are believed to represent the Jew and the Gentile, united in Messiah. The loaves were held up before the Lord by the priest in the Temple. There he performed a wave offering in every direction to God so the remainder of the harvest would be blessed. The book of Joel speaks that the restoration of Israel will occur during the season of the Spring harvest. This event, the redemption and restoration of Israel, occurred on the 20th day of the counting of the Omer on May 14, 1948. In the Scripture, the number twenty always presents redemption; so the people and land of Israel were redeemed by God and the nation was restored after 2,000 years.

All of Yeshua Jesus' appearances after the resurrection occurred during the counting of the Omer. On the fortieth day of the counting, which represents "new beginnings", Yeshua Jesus told his disciples to wait in Jerusalem for what His Father promised [the Holy Spirit] – Acts 1:4. Acts 1:9 says, "And after He had said these things, He was lifted up while they were looking on, and a cloud received Him out of their sight". This is known as the Ascension. It is interesting that on Pentecost, man was given the gift of the indwelling of the Holy Spirit and on Shavuot, during the Jewish celebration on the same day, Israel was given God's instructions which are translated as Laws. The scripture tells us when the law was given that the heavenly shofar sounded loud and long. This type of sound is called the Great Teruah. When the Great Teruah is blown, the one blowing the shofar blows it as loud and long as he can. Both the giving of the Law and the gift of the Holy Spirit occurred on the same day, one thousand years apart. Pentecost is the day when the Old Testament and the New Testament were jointed together as one.

To the Jews: Shavuot is a memorial of when God gave the Torah to Moses on Mount Sinai fifty days after the Jewish people had left Egypt.

To the Christians: Pentecost marks the supernatural birth of the church. It was the day our Lord sent the promised Holy Spirit to His disciples while they waited in Jerusalem after Yeshua' resurrection. It appeared as flames of fire over their heads. This "baptism of the Holy Spirit" helped them to become more effective witnesses in the world to who Messiah Yeshua is. It also increased their ability to share the Good News with others as a result of their receiving an ability to speak in one of the seventy languages in the world at that time. Dr. Chuck Missler believes "it is likely that the Rapture of the church will occur on the birthday of the church". Pentecost may then represent the end of the harvest for Gentile believers as God turns His focus on the Jews once more.

Exodus 19:16-20 describes how God presented the Torah to Moses. It says: "So it came about on the third day, when it was morning, that there were thunder and lightning flashes and a thick cloud upon the mountain and a very loud trumpet sound, so that all the people who were in the camp trembled. And Moses brought the people out of the camp to meet God, and they stood at the foot of the mountain. Now Mount Sinai was all in smoke because the Lord descended upon it in fire; and its smoke ascended like the smoke of a furnace, and the whole mountain quaked violently. When the sound of the trumpet grew louder and louder, Moses spoke and God answered him with thunder. The Lord came down on Mount Sinai, to the top of the mountain, and the Lord called Moses to the top of the mountain, and Moses went up".

The Scriptures speak in these verses about the sound of the trumpet that grew louder and louder. We know the trumpet mentioned here is referring to the shofar. We learn the sound of the shofar is associated with thunder and the voice of God in Exodus 19:13. It says: ... 'When the ram's horn sounds a long blast, they shall come up to the mountain'. Who are "they"? God is referring to the children of Israel and other elite Egyptians who came with them when they left Egypt. These were the group of people who were to stand at the foot of the mountain where they would meet with God. They were not to go up to the top. Only Moses was instructed to meet with God there. Psalm 29:3-9 also speaks about the awesome power of the voice of God. Verse 4, 7 says: The voice of the Lord is powerful, the voice of the Lord is majestic ... The voice of the Lord hews out flames of fire.

Note: What is believed to be the actual mountain described in the Exodus account as Mount Sinai has been located. It was found in a barren desert area of Saudi Arabia, not on the Egyptian Sinai Peninsula as was previously thought. Today the 8,000 foot high granite mountain is called Jabal Al Lawz. Both the mount of Horeb and Mount Sinai connect at the base of the Lawz mountain range. It is the only mountain in the area where the top is the color of charcoal. It is an interesting observation that the entire mountain range is surrounded by high barbed-wire fences and patrolled by armed guards. One has to wonder why. Photographs of the mountain were secretly smuggled out of Saudi Arabia. They line-up precisely with the biblical account of the Hebrews as they journeyed toward the Promised Land and Moses' encounter with God on the top of a mountain where he received the Ten Words [Ten Commandments]. This finding proves the Scriptures to be very accurate when one follows the directions of the location as written.

Michael Norton wrote that according to oral tradition, the children of Israel "saw sound waves in the form of fiery substances [as they waited at the bottom of the mountain]. Each commandment, as it left God's mouth, circled the whole camp and eventually rested on each Jew personally". The people also said they heard God's voice in many different languages. This sounds like a parallel for what occurred on Pentecost that was recorded in Acts 2:2-6.

Dr. Richard Booker wrote, "Jewish scholars believe that the people actually 'saw the voice of God coming out of the mountain in tongues of fire'. The mixed multitude that came out of Egypt saw the tongues of fire and heard the one voice of God speak in their different languages so they could understand His words". This pattern is repeated in the book of Acts when the disciples were blessed with the indwelling of the Holy Spirit which appeared as flames of fire over their heads and which gave them the ability to speak in one of seventy languages spoken in the world during that time.

Why did God select this particular time to pour out His spirit on the disciples? Because, Jews from many nations were required to be in Jerusalem at this time to celebrate the Feast of Shavuot. This outpouring is known as "the early/later rain". The "former rain" occurs in the Fall. The scripture tells us that the people were amazed when they heard the Good News proclaimed in their own language by these uneducated disciples. It was an undeniable miracle. This miracle changed the history of the world by supernaturally birthing the church. It is estimated about one quarter of the Jews believed the message they heard.

There is a prophecy in the book of Joel that also connects to this event and others like it that follows. Joel 2: 28-29 says: "It will come about after this [the years the locust have eaten] that I will pour out My Spirit on all mankind; and your sons and daughters will prophesy, your old men will dream dreams, your young men will see visions. Even on the male and female servants I will Pour out My Spirit in those days.

The book of Genesis gives us an interesting insight into the Holy Spirit which is represented by a dove. When Noah let the raven [and unclean bird] out of the ark for the first time, it did not return with an olive branch in its mouth, but "flew here and there until the water was dried up from the earth" –Genesis 8:7. Some associate the raven with Satan who goes back and forth over the earth looking for someone to devour – II Peter 5:8. The second time Noah released a dove, it returned with the olive branch which showed the earth was now dry land. The olive trees survived the flood because they are known to have very deep roots. Some believe this second release and return of the dove represents Israel today. Many Jews, especially the young ones, are accepting Yeshua as their Messiah. As a result, there are currently over a hundred Messianic Fellowships in the land of Israel. While many Jews continue to reject Yeshua as their Messiah, those that do will sadly go through the Tribulation Period and many will find Him at the end.

Ruth: A Gentile in the Genealogy of the Messiah

The story of Ruth is read every year at Shavuot in the schools and synagogues around the world. In this book, the ancient meanings behind Ruth and Boaz's actions were clarified using the Complete Jewish Study Bible. The story of Ruth illustrates the importance of loyalty and redemption. Ruth was from the country of Moab which was located in what is now the country of Jordan. She was a descendent of Lot and his two daughters, and the cousin of Rebekah. The third chapter of the book of Judges mentions her grandfather Eglon. He was the King of Moab. As a Moabite woman, Ruth was a Gentile. The Scripture says she loved her mother-in-law Naomi and chose to remain with her when Naomi returned to Bethlehem from Moab. It must have been a difficult decision for Ruth to leave everything she had known behind as the granddaughter of a king. Her willingness to travel to a foreign land with a different culture shows the deep level of love and commitment Ruth felt for Naomi. It would also indicate what a special woman Naomi was and how God was working behind the scene in the lives of both of these women to accomplish His will. Their decision to leave Moab appears historically to have corresponded with a terrible famine in the land. As a result of the famine there were probably many desperate people traveling by foot on the road in search of food elsewhere. This situation would also have drawn robbers in search of booty from the pilgrim groups. We do not know if Naomi and her daughter-in-law started out on the journey alone or if they where with a group of people for safety. If the women were traveling alone this journey would have been particularly dangerous for them.

Naomi and Ruth arrived in Bethlehem in early Spring, at the time of the barley harvest. They were very poor, and both were widows. Naomi had a wealthy kinsman, named Boaz. He saw Ruth as she gleaned in his field for their food. Boaz was very kind to her because of how she cared for Naomi. He asked her not to glean in anyone else's field but his. This action, in a footnote on Chapter 2:8-10 in The Complete Jewish Study Bible indicates that "he adopted her as part of Naomi's family, thus granting her privileges usually accorded only to a family member within the house of Israel". Studies have shown that he gave her pita bread and hummus, not vinegar as some believed. One evening at the end of the harvest, Ruth secretly uncovered Boaz' feet as Naomi had suggested and laid by them as he slept. The Complete Jewish Study Bible describes in a footnote that this action by Ruth was her wedding proposal to Boaz. Boaz wanted Ruth as his wife but there was another family member closer than he was to Naomi's deceased husband. According to the ancient Jewish law recorded in Deuteronomy 23:5-10 an unmarried man was required to marry the widow of his closest male relative in order to produce a child with her. This marriage was called a Levirate marriage. Its purpose was so the deceased husband's name would remain in Israel and his wife would be well cared for. Boaz went to the City Gate, Chapter 4:1, and asked ten of the city's leaders to sit with him. Boaz wanted them to serve as witnesses when he asked the closest relative if he was willing to marry Ruth. If the man declined, he would take off his sandal and gave it to Boaz. Since the other relative declined the offer, the deal was sealed concerning who would be Ruth's kinsman redeemer. The removed sandal is referred to as the halitzah sandal, which means "taking off the shoe". In this manner, Boaz redeemed Ruth and became her kinsman redeemer which is called a "go'el" in Hebrew. He married Ruth during the time of the grain harvest in late Summer. Therefore, Boaz, the Jew, redeemed Ruth and took her as his Gentile bride, just as the Messiah has a Gentile bride as well as Jews that make up members of His family. It is believed that Ruth converted to Judaism when she told Naomi "your God will be my God". She bore Boaz a son whom they named Obed. Obed was the grandfather of King David and is in the lineage of Yeshua Jesus, the Messiah. The story shows that God in His sovereignty works in the lives of those who are faithful to Him despite the unfaithfulness of His chosen people, Israel.

One of the most exciting things this writer saw while on a tour of the Shepherd's Field in Bethlehem was the ruins of what is believed to be the home of Ruth and Boaz. Seeing it proved once more the accuracy of their story as recorded in the Scriptures.

How Shavuot is Celebrated in Israel Today

The Jewish people decorate their homes on Shavuot with flowers, green plants and basket of fruits to represent the harvest. They also wear bright clothing.

This story is read every year by Jewish children with their teachers in their schools and in the synagogues. The people reflect on King David and the town in which he was born. They imagine what it must have been like to be in Bethlehem at the time of King David and see the fields of grain bowing down in the warm Summer breeze. The boys probably imagine the sound of the scythe as the grain was being cut and willowed and try to sense the sweet smell of fresh cut sheaves. The girls probably imagine themselves being Ruth as she gleaned from the corners of Boaz' field or as she laid herself at Boaz' feet after the harvest was completed. They may imagine uncovering the feet of their future husband just as Ruth uncovered the feet of Boaz as he slept which was Ruth's way of asking Boaz to marry her!

Gary Stearman says that religious Jews hold a vigil of prayer and study all night in their synagogues on Shavuot. He says, "the Jews stay up all night studying... small sections from each book of the Torah, [the book of Ruth], and the Talmud, representing all of the most important texts of Judaism in their synagogues.... The sense of preparation for Sinai is heightened by a mystical tradition holding that the skies open up during this night for a brief instant. In that very moment God will favorably answer any prayer". Stearman also believes "the day is marked in heaven as a day of judgment for the fruit of the trees".

A Personal Story: The Baptism of the Holy Spirit

There is a debate in the modern church concerning the baptism of the Holy Spirit. Some denominations believe that the indwelling of the Holy Spirit was for that one specific time in history. Other denominations believe the indwelling is for today since God is the same yesterday, today, and forever. I can personally testify that those denominations that do not believe this gift is for believers in the present Age, are incorrect.

I had heard of the "baptism of the Holy Spirit" early in my Christian walk. It was a gift I desired and sought so I could experience everything that God had to give to His children. I was going through a difficult time in my life and I just wanted more of God to fill me with His love. One day I drove over to my best friend's home. She was a Pentecostal Pastor and very gifted in the Scriptures. I shared with her my desire to receive the baptism of the Holy Spirit, and the fact that I had no idea what I had to do to receive it. A few days later she invited me over for dinner. When I arrived I was surprised to see that several other pastors were in attendance. After dinner, as we talked, I shared with them my desire to connect with God spiritually on a deeper level. They said, lets pray. For several hours we prayed – me quietly in English with my hands raised to heaven, and they in their spiritual language. After awhile, one of the pastors whispered something into my ear. To this day I can't tell you what he said to me, but I believe it had something to do with my ministry. Around midnight, we decided to say our farewells since it was getting late. Nothing seemed different to me. I got into my car to drive home. When I was about half way home, all of the sudden I found myself praying in another language; a language that was foreign to me. I had no idea what I was saying but I felt an overwhelming joy! Tears began to flow from my eyes! I couldn't believe it! I spent the rest of my short journey home praising God and thanking Him for the beautiful gift He bestowed upon me. After arriving home, I continued praising Him until 3 a.m. When I crawled into bed I instantly fell into a deep sleep. When I awoke in the morning, I heard a menacing voice say, "You can't speak in tongues"! I knew instantly that it was the devil's voice! I spoke out, "Yes I can you devil! Get out of here"! I knew darkness could never overcome light, but that light could always overcome and destroy darkness. He never attacked me in the same way again. But I know he is, as the scripture says, a roaring lion looking for someone to devour. It was a test he lost.

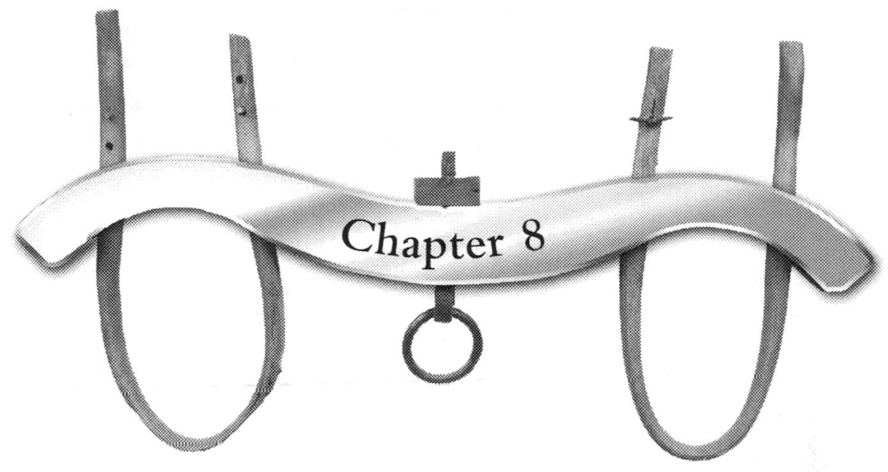

The Fall Feasts Begin with Trumpets/Rosh Hashanah

The season of the Fall Feasts begins with the sounding of the trumpets [shofar] on the Feast of Trumpets. In modern Israel, this feast represents the beginning of the civil year. The Fall new year was adapted by the Jews during their bondage in Babylon. Up to that point they celebrated the New Year in the Spring, on Nisan 1, as God had commanded them. Additionally, it is thought by some to be "an annual re-coronation of God as the King of the world" and the day Adam was created by God.

With the arrival of Rosh Hashanah [the civil new year], the Jews began to prepare for the most holy and somber day of the year, Yom Kippur. From Rosh Hashanah to Yom Kippur the Jews have a ten day period of penitence called the "Days of Awe". When Yom Kippur arrives, the Jews believe the books of God are opened and that the people are judged according to the deeds they performed during the past year. They are hopeful that their good deeds will outweigh the bad so they will be acceptable to God and their names will be written in the Book of Life for another year. Less than a week after Yom Kippur comes the Feast of Tabernacles. It is the last harvest feast of the year. The Jewish people are joyful. They are happy they have made it through Yom Kippur and are celebrating another year. The Feast of Tabernacles has several names. It is also called the "Feast of Ingathering" which is when the fruits of the harvest are picked and sold or stored and the "Feast of Homecoming". The Jewish people are continuing to return to their ancestral land of Israel after 2,000 years of dispersion. The Christian church is returning to its Jewish roots and many Jews are accepting Yeshua Jesus as their Messiah. The final ingathering will consist of both Jews and Gentiles who have accepted Yeshua Jesus as Messiah and Savior at the end of the age.

The Feast of Trumpets/Rosh Hashanah/The Hidden Day

Rosh Hashanah means "the head of the year". It is the first of three Fall Feasts that will be fulfilled by Yeshua at His Second Coming. It is called by many names: Rosh Hashanah, the New Year, the Feast of Yom Teruah, Day of Blowing, Day of the Awakening Blast, Yom HaDin: Day of Judgment, the Opening of the Books, the Opening of the Gates, and Yom HaKeseh: The Hidden Day, Ha Melech: the Coronation of the Messiah, the Feast of Trumpets and the Time of Jacob's Trouble. It is often called Yom Teruah in the Jewish community. Yom Teruah means "the day of the blast". Teruah is one of the notes on the shofar. It consists of a sequence of nine short blasts. While the ancient Jewish people did not understand the purpose of this memorial, they celebrated it as a memorial to Creation. Some rabbis believe that God began His work of Creation on a Sunday. In Hebrew the word for creation means "day one". Sunday is the first day after the Sabbath, so it is day one. Some ancient texts connect Rosh Hashanah with the sighting of the new moon when signal fires were set on hilltops to announce its arrival. They believed the new moon was sanctified. If Rosh Hashanah fell on a Sabbath, the shofar would be blown in the temple, but not elsewhere. The rabbis believed if one blew the shofar outside of the temple on a Sabbath they would be engaging in work, and to do any work on the Sabbath was strictly forbidden.

The Feast of Trumpets 11 is a holy convocation [Sabbath] that is held in the Hebrew month of Tishri. During this holy convocation, the blowing of the shofar is made up of a grouping of thirty sounds repeated twice and a single grouping of ten blasts Leviticus 23:23-25 says: And again the Lord spoke to Moses, saying, "Speak to the sons of Israel, saying, 'In the seventh month on the first of the month you shall have a rest, a reminder by blowing of trumpets, a holy convocation. You shall not do any laborious work, but you shall present an offering by fire to the Lord.'" The date of the Feast of Trumpets on the Julian calendar is usually between the end of September and early October. It is the beginning of ten days of self-examination and penitence by the Jewish people in preparation for Yom Kippur. These ten days are known as the Days of Awe. The trumpet that is blown during this feast is a shofar or ram's horn. It was blown 100X during the day of convocation to announce the arrival of the new moon. This was the only feast that occurred over two different but consecutive days. It was dependent on when the news of the new moon's appearance reached the Jewish communities outside of Jerusalem. Because of the time it took to get the news in ancient days, no one knew the day or the hour the new moon would appear.

The shofar or trumpet was traditionally blown only by the Levitical priests and the watchmen. The priests blew the shofar to announce a sacred assembly. The watchman blew the shofar to warn the people in times of danger.

To the Jews: The shofar was blown in remembrance of the ram that was sacrificed in place of Isaac recorded in Genesis 22:13. It is the day when the Books of Life are opened. The sounding blast of the shofar on the year of Jubilee calls the sons of Israel back to his inheritance and back to his family. It is a year of freedom. Messianic Jews look for the Rapture of the church to occur at the time of this feast.

To the Christians: Many Christians believe that the Rapture of the church will take place on the 100th blast of the shofar on the Feast of Trumpets on some year. At the sound of that last trump, the children of God will immediately join the Lord in the air and will forever be with the Lord – I Thessalonians 4:16-17. The Rapture is known as the day of the Lord. It will occur suddenly, in a twinkling of an eye, as a thief in the night – I Thessalonians 5:2.

Events around the Feast of Trumpets

The Feast of Trumpets marks nine important events:

1. One of the most important events on the Feast of Trumpets in the Jewish community is that it marks the first day of the opening of the Book of Life. This book determines who will live and who will die during the coming year based on a person's good deeds and acts of repentance. The Jewish people seem to lack knowledge of the warning in Isaiah 64:6 that says, "all our righteous deeds are like a filthy garment" to God; and that a blood covering is required to be redeemed.
2. It is the day the Lord God created the earth and Adam opened his eyes for the first time in the Garden of Eden. It is believed by the Sages that the first voice Adam heard was the voice of God saying, "I Am the Lord Your God".
3. It is the day when Messiah Yeshua will be crowned King of Kings and Lord of Lords. His coronation psalm is Psalm 47:1-2, 5-8. This speaks of events before the war of Gog and Magog.
4. It is the day the shofar sounds 100X and at the last blast, the Rapture of the church may take place.
5. The blast of the shofar is an appeal to the listener to contemplate their transgressions and is a call for repentance.
6. The period of time between the birth of the church in the Summer during Pentecost and the Feast of Trumpets when the harvest is completed in the Fall, represents the age of the Gentile church
7. This marks the beginning of Jacob's Trouble also known as the Tribulation Period – Jeremiah 30:7.
8. It is the only feast that falls on a new moon.
9. The Jews believe the sounding of the shofar on Rosh Hashanah confounds Satan and renders him powerless against the Jews plea for forgiveness.

The Shofar's Call

Jewish commentaries point out that the shofar is evidence of freedom. It is made from the hollowed horns of four different animals: the ram's horn, an antelope horn, a large Yemenite Kudu's horn, or more recently from the horn of an ancient sheep known as Jacob's sheep. The restoration of this type of sheep in Israel is a fulfillment of Ezekiel's prophecy concerning the last days.

The shofar as a musical instrument is similar to a modern day bugle. It is believed to be the only musical instrument from ancient Israel that has survived in its original form and is still used today. Since God could not speak directly to His people without terrifying them, He chose to spoke indirectly through the use of the shofar. Amos 3:6 says: "Shall a shofar be blown in a city and the people not tremble". Once the shofar is blown on the Sabbath or the feast days everything that follows it is considered sacred in the presence of the Lord. The only time it is blown daily is during the month of Elul, the month for repentance, when the Lord is in the field.

The ram's horn is first mentioned in Genesis concerning the offering of Isaac to God by Abraham. According to the story, just when Abraham was about to slay his only son Isaac, who was thirty-seven years old at the time, an angel of the Lord stopped him. Genesis 22:13 says, "then Abraham raised his eyes and looked, and behold, behind him a ram caught in the thicket by his horns; and Abraham went and took the ram and offered him up for a burnt offering in the place of his son". Some people believe that Abraham's faith in God was so strong that he knew if Isaac died, God would raise him from the dead, just as He would Yeshua, His only son, generations later. It is interesting that after this event, Sarah no longer lived in the same town with Abraham. Some suggest that Sarah was so angry at Abraham for his actions toward Isaac that she left Abraham and moved to the town of Hebron where she lived until her death. Biltz said she moved to Hebron because that is where she was told by an angel that she would have a son.

Two types of trumpets, not just the shofar [ram's horn], were originally used in the temple in Jerusalem. Numbers 10:2-3 describes the silver horns that were used. The two silver trumpets were made from the half shekel coins that were required to be given to the priests as a temple tax. Silver represents redemption before God by God's redeemed people. A golden trumpet was blown on the year on the Jubilee. Jubilee occurred on the 50th year following the Shemitah of 7x7 or 49 years.

<u>**Note:**</u> Two talented musicians from El Shaddai Ministries in Tacoma, WA have demonstrated the various sounds and lengths of the sounds of the shofar. Not only is the shofar blown on the Feast of Trumpets, but also during other appropriate feast days and weekly to welcome in the Sabbath. The shofar consists of nine notes and three sounds. All have specific meanings.

The word **Tekia** means "to stop or pause". It consists of a single long sustained blast. It is as if God is asking His people to stop what they are doing and focus on Him. It also shows God's sovereign rule over the earth, the people on the earth, and on the territories over which it is blown.

A **Great Tekia** is a prolonged Tekia in which the shofar blower holds the note for as long as he can. It represents the sound of joy and announces that the king has arrived!

A **Teruah** is a sequence of nine quick blasts in short succession. It is meant to wake us up from our spiritual slumber. It sounds similar to an alarm clock when it signals the approaching danger in war, or when it orders men to attack using God's strategies. An The book of Joshua gives us an example how it is used. In Joshua 6 the Lord tells Joshua to march his troops around the city of Jericho for six days, and on the seventh day to march around the city seven times. As a result of obeying God, Joshua and his men won the battle. The walls of Jericho fell on the seventh day as the trumpet blew and the people shouted. When we obey God, He releases us into His purpose and into our future, just as He did in the Battle of Jericho. The blasts are also associated with repentance.

The word **Shevarim** means "to be broken and is a sound of repentance". It is a sequence of three short blasts that mimics the playing of a trumpet. It breaks down any resistance one may have to the Lord and allows God's power, grace, and purposes to be accomplished on earth. It leads God's people to victory whether they are against a person, group of enemies, or a territory. It was used to break through enemy lines and to cause confusion in an enemies' camp. Dr. Mike Evans has written that "some people have said this sound resembles the cries of a man yearning to connect with Jehovah and believe it is the cry of a 'broken spirit; a broken and contrite heart'". Thus in this case it is considered to be a sound associated with pain and grief.

Prior to the destruction of the holy Temple in Jerusalem large orchestras containing many musicians with different instruments played during the Sabbath services in the Temple. Their music seemed to connect with the spirit of God and promoted a sense of happiness and peace among those attending religious services. One needs only to reflect on the scriptures about King Saul; how he was soothed when David played the harp for him. After the holy Temple in Jerusalem was destroyed, the shofar became the primary instrument played during temple services. The sounds of the shofar continues to remind the Jewish people of their duties to serve God, their instruction to honor life as holy and precious, and when God provided a ram caught in a thicket to be offered by Abraham as a sacrifice in place of his son Isaac on Mount Moriah.

As noted, the shofar served many purposes; both secular and

religious. In the past, only two groups of people were allowed to blow the shofar; the Levitical priests and the watchman. The watchman was posted on the walls of the city or in a watchtower. It was his job to warn the people in the city of impending danger from an enemy. Today the shofar is primarily associated with the Sabbath, Rosh Hashanah, and the Year of Jubilee. It is the sound of God's victory, God's deliverance, and God's reigning. It continues to be sounded in the period between Rosh Codesh (the new moon) on the ninth of Elul until after Yom Kippur. In ancient Israel only the Levitical priests were allowed to perform the religious functions of blowing the shofar in the Jewish Commonwealth.

Religious uses: The Scripture tells us that the shofar was used in the transfer of the Ark of the Covenant, it announced the New Moon each month, and was/is blown during the Feast days of Rosh Hashanah, Yom Kippur, and the Feast of Tabernacles. It was blown in the Water Libation ceremony, to mark the end of a festival, and during the Year of Jubilee which occurs every 50th year after seven Shemitah years of seven years each. It is also blown to welcome in the Sabbath and to gather God's people together to meet with God. The Jews believe that when the 100 blasts are blown, the gates of heaven are opened.

Secular uses included: the coronation of the king, a warning during times of drought and pestilence, signaling in times of war or danger, to assemble troops to pursue, attack, and to proclaim victory over their enemies. In the end times it will call for Israel to gather together in Zion. We are now witnessing the Jews return to Zion since Israel was restored as a nation in 1948 after 2,000 years of dispersion around the globe.

The Shofar and the Watchman

In ancient Israel a watchman was assigned a position on a high wall of the city or in watchtowers to watch and warn the people of impending danger or war. His job was critical to the safety of the inhabitants in the city. They were to protect the city and its people from harm during the day hours and during the night hours from their enemies. Isaiah 62:6 says: "On your wall, O Jerusalem, I have appointed watchmen; all day and all night they will never keep silent".

The word watchman in Hebrew means "one who looks up". A watchman had to be vigilant and have excellent eyesight since it was his responsibility to keep the city and its inhabitants safe. They could not rest or go into the city to enjoy the entertainment available there when on duty. Each watchman had to stay focused and on his post at all times. He was their civil defense system! When or if he saw danger approaching the city he would blow the shofar as a warning to wake the people up so they could prepare to defend themselves. Once the watchman sounded a warning, his job was done. Ezekiel 33:3-4, 6 speaks of the how critical the Lord considers the watchman's duty to be. It says "[If a watchman] sees the sword coming upon the land and blows on the trumpet and warns the people; then he who hears the sound of the trumpet and does not take warning, and a sword comes and takes him away, his blood will be on his own head....but if the watchman see the sword coming and does not blow the trumpet and the people are not warned, and a sword comes and takes a person from them, he is taken away in his iniquity; but his blood I will require from the watchman's hand"'.

Does the role of a watchman apply in our day?

Absolutely yes! Everyone who believes in Messiah is a watchman. We are watching for the return of the Lord and the Rapture of the church. We know that time is short, so we must stay alert. Signs of the Lord's imminent return are all around us and the harvest is coming to a close. Our job as believers therefore is to wake people up to the fact that the Lord is coming soon. We must share the Gospel of Messiah with them before it is too late. We must not put off for tomorrow what needs to be done today. The enemy is trying to steal the souls of people and the love of many has grown cold. In some European countries only 1-2% of the people are believers in Messiah! In America only about 30% of the Millennials are believers! Recently a television host said Christian beliefs were a mental illness! The enemy Satan battles against God's people as he appears deceptively as an angel of light. We, as watchmen, must remain strong and fight the good fight. We must intercede and pray for the lost, and share with them how much God loves them. For each person who repents, the Bible says all the angels in heaven rejoice with singing! Each person who responds positively to the Gospel message is a soul that is pulled away from Satan's grasp and away from eternal damnation. Joel 2:1-2 says: "Blow a trumpet [shofar] in Zion, and sound an alarm on My holy mountain! Let all the inhabitants of the land tremble, for the day of the Lord is coming, surely it is near. A day of darkness and gloom, a day of clouds and thick darkness. As the dawn is spread over the mountains, so there is a great and strong people; there has never been anything like it, nor will there be again after it, to the years of many generations".

How Rosh Hashanah is Celebrated By Jews Today

Rosh Hashanah marks the civil Jewish new year and is the day that begins the Ten Days of Awe which lead to Yom Kippur. One of the ways the Jews celebrate this feast, after attending a Sabbath service, is by eating apples and challah bread dipped in honey with their family and friends. This is their way of wishing everyone a sweet New Year. Some Jews eat different or unfamiliar types of fruit on this day while others chose to fast. Some take pilgrimages while others exchange messages of love and good wishes to friends and family both near and far.

One major problem with the new year being celebrated in the Fall is that the Fall is a time of endings and not a time of new life. Most importantly is the fact that Rosh Hashanah is not being celebrated on the month God told the Jewish people to celebrate their new year on. He told them that their new year was to be celebrated on the first day on the month of Nisan [also called Abib] on the Jewish calendar [usually during early April on the Julian calendar]. God wanted His people to celebrate at a time different from the other nations around them; during the time when the trees and flowers bud and many animals give birth to their young. This timing would fit perfectly in the pattern God had established that points to the birth of His son, the Messiah. However, between the writing of the Torah and the codification of the oral teaching of Judaism, Rosh Hashanah became recognized as the new year. Additionally, in order to solve the problem between what God said and when the nations around them celebrated the new year, the Jewish sages created two calendars – a civil calendar and a religious one. The rabbis justified having two new year celebrations by saying there is a lot more than one new year. They used the celebration of the new year of trees – Tu B'Shevat – as an example.

Day of Atonement/Yom Kippur

Yom Kippur is one of the most solemn feasts on the Jewish calendar. It is the second of the Fall Feasts that Yeshua Jesus will fulfill at the time of His Second Coming. He began His ministry on Yom Kippur during His First Coming during a Jubilee year. Many religious scholars believe He will return to earth on Yom Kippur from heaven at His Second Coming. Pastor Biltz believes the Second Coming will occur toward the end of the Tribulation Period. He bases this on Revelation 19:2, 13-15. According to Isaiah 61:2 when He returns, it will be "the day of vengeance of our God". Prophetically, on this day, Israel as a nation will realize Yeshua Jesus is their Messiah.

The first Day of Atonement occurred forty days after the people sinned against God by worshipping the golden calf. After the people's grievous sin, Moses returned to Mount Sinai to ask God to forgive His people and accept their atonement for their sins. When Moses went up the mountain the first time, he was gone so long the people thought he had died. As a result, they reverted back to worshipping the golden calf, one of the gods of Egypt. When Moses returned and saw what was happening, he was furious with Aaron whom he had left in charge of the people in his absence. Aaron had no excuse. Moses had given Aaron a hand written copy of the covenant he had copied from the mouth of God. Because the people had broken their covenant with

God, Moses threw down the Ten Words, commonly known as the Ten Commandments, God had written on a tablet of stone and broke them in front of the people. It is said these tablets were translucent and could be read from either side. It is important to understand that Moses did not throw down the Ten Words given to him by God in anger as is often depicted in pictures or taught in churches. The common practice of that day was for a person to destroy a legal contract in the place it was made with another person, if the other person had fulfilled their agreement. Moses was holding a legal contract between the nation of Israel and God. When he broke the contract in front of the entire nation, his action showed that the contract had been annulled. This public action let both parties involved in the agreement know that the agreement was destroyed. Deuteronomy 9:17-18 supports this suggestion that Moses was simply following the protocol of the time. It says: "I took hold of the two tablets and threw them from my hands and smashed them before your eyes. I threw them down before the Lord, ...".

When Moses returned to Mount Sinai again to speak to God on behalf of the children of Israel, he asked God to forgive their sins and not destroy them. Exodus 32:32 reveals to us Moses' request before God. It says, "But now, if You will forgive their sin ---- and if not, please blot me out from Your book which You have written". Pastor Biltz pointed out the lines after Moses said "if not, please blot me out ---- and if not" shows Moses had paused and was contemplating what he would say next. This pause is not found in any other place in the Scriptures. When one sees this verse in Hebrew, Moses' name is blotted out of the verse! Before and after that verse only Aaron's name is mentioned in this chapter! Forty days later, Moses returned to the people with a new set of "Ten Words" which he placed in an ark of acacia wood he had made. When the people saw Moses, they knew their sins had been atoned for. The Lord instructed Moses to tell the people to keep this holy convocation in Leviticus 23: 26-31. It says: The Lord spoke to Moses, saying, "On exactly the tenth day of this seventh month is the day of atonement; it shall be a holy convocation for you, and you shall humble your souls and present an offering by fire to the Lord. You shall not do any work on this same day, for it is a day of atonement, to make atonement on your behalf before the Lord your God. If there is any person who will not humble himself on this same day, he shall be cut off from his people. As for any person who does any work on this same day, that person I will destroy from among his people. You shall do no work at all. It is to be a perpetual statute throughout your generations in all your dwelling places".

Six Important Things from Leviticus 23:26-31.

First, Yom Kippur is to be held exactly on the tenth day of the seventh month.
Second, the people are to humble their souls.
Third, they are to present an offering by fire to the Lord. In this offering the whole animal is consumed and is the only offering totally dedicated to the Lord.
Fourth, Work is forbidden on this day. If a person works God will destroy him from among his people.
Fifth, It is a day to make atonement on your behalf before the Lord.
Sixth, If a person does not humble themselves on this day, he will be cut off from his people.

God takes this day so seriously that if someone does not humble himself or chooses to work on this day, they will be cut off from their people.

Seven days before Yom Kippur the High Priest was taken away from his house and sequestered in a room in the Sanhedrin chamber of the Temple called the Chamber of Hewn Stone. It is believed that by the second temple period the High Priest was no longer required to be a Levite. He was given the position as a political appointee. As such he often was ignorant of the functions or rituals that could be performed only by the High Priest. Since the High Priest played a critical role in the performance of the rituals in the temple, Jewish elders would instruct him about his duties for Yom Kippur so that he could perform them correctly. He was given no food the night before Yom Kippur to assist him in staying awake. If he did fall asleep and by chance have a seminal emission, he would be defiled and ineligible to officiate the following day. This was very serious since the people's lives and the fate of the nation were dependent on how the ceremony was conducted before the Lord. The climax of this holiest day of the year was when the High Priest went into the Holy of Holies. There he made an animal sacrifice for himself, for his family, the Levites, and for the sins of the nation. He burned incense and prayed a brief prayer to God. Meanwhile the people waited with anticipation for the High Priest to re-appear. They feared that the actions of the High Priest may have in some way offended God and resulted in his being killed until they saw him emerge from behind the curtain which separated the Holy of Holies from the Holy Place. They knew if God accepted their atonement they would have a new beginning. If not, their names would be blotted out of the Book of Life.

God clearly illustrates the consequence of disobedience in the story of Jonah. This story is read on every Yom Kippur as a reminder to the people of the importance of obeying God's commands. The story begins with God commanding Jonah to go to Nineveh to warn the people of impending destruction unless they repented from their sins. Jonah was afraid to go to Nineveh because the Assyrians, who were very wicked and cruel people, ruled from there. So Jonah decided to run away to Tarshish. [This is never a good idea!] He found a ship that was going to Tarshish, paid the fare and went down into it to go with them to Tarshish from the presence of the Lord – Jonah 1: 3. Little did he know that the Lord had prepared a great fish to swallow Jonah up because of his failure to obey God's command. On the way to Tarshish, the Lord sent a strong wind and the seas roared to the point that the sailors became frightened for their lives. They asked Jonah why he brought evil upon them. When he told them he was running away from God they became even more terrified. They asked him what they could do to calm the sea and he told them to throw him into the sea. Once in the sea a fish swallowed him up. Jonah prayed while three days in the belly of the fish for the Lord to spare him, and "then the Lord commanded the fish, and it vomited Jonah up onto the dry land – Jonah 2:10. The Lord told Jonah a second time to go to Nineveh. This time Jonah obeyed the Lord, even though he had to walk 500 miles to reach Nineveh! Jonah warned the people that in forty days the city would be destroyed if they did not repent. The people believed God and repented. This greatly displeased Jonah! He went outside of the city and sat on its east side ... He hoped God would change His mind despite the fact that he knew God was a God of compassion who would spare the people as a result of their repentance.

Why did the people of Ninevah repent? Because God had prepared them to receive Jonah's warning by allowing them to first experience two plagues, a civil war, and a solar eclipse! As a result, they were ready to listen. Jonah did not want God to have compassion on Nineveh because of how evil the Assyrians of Ninevah were, yet he accepted that God showed him mercy by delivering him from the evil he did. Pastor Biltz says: "The power of your repentance is not that it changes your past but you are saying you are changing the future. True repentance is a change of heart, mind and behavior". That is what the ten Days of Awe are all about.

The ten days between the Rosh Hashanah/Trumpets and Yom Kippur/Atonement are called the "Days of Awe" or "Days of Repentance". The Jews believe that God writes every person's words, deeds, and thoughts in His book. They hope their good deeds and charity will outnumber their sinful deeds so their name will be inscribed in the book of life for another year. When the tenth day arrives, according to tradition, three books are opened. Sam Nadler described them as follows: There is a book for the "absolutely wicked", one for the "perfectly righteous", and one for "ordinary people". After the books are opened on Rosh Hashanah/Feast of Trumpets, the people have ten days to do good deeds to merit being placed in the Book of Life for the coming year. On Yom Kippur judgment is made. After the judgments are made, a name is put into one of the three books. The books are then closed for one year.

I use to wonder why a name would be written in the book only one year at a time. I now understand without the blood of Yeshua Jesus which takes away the sin once and for all of those who believe in Him, there is no redemption. The Jewish people have been partially blinded to who Messiah Yeshua is at this point, just as the Gentile has been partially blinded to the Torah. Without the atoning blood of Yeshua Jesus, and with no temple in which to offer God the blood sacrifices of animals, the Jewish people are substituting works for atonement. In reality, they have no means of forgiveness or redemption without first accepting Yeshua Jesus. Before His death, the blood of one year old lambs and bulls was used as a temporary covering and the sacrifices needed to be performed in the Holy of Holies by the High Priest yearly. With the sacrifice of Yeshua Jesus on our behalf, all the sins of believers in Him have been forgiven as though they never happened and have been removed for eternity. He became our sin offering, our atonement. The Scripture says, though your sins be as scarlet, they will be as white as wool when you are under the saving grace of Yeshua's sacrifice.

To the Jews: Yom Kippur is the holiness day of the year in all of Judaism. It is believed that some day on Yom Kippur a final judgment and accounting will be made of a person's soul and the person's future will be sealed for eternity. Since the destruction of the temple in Jerusalem in 70 AD the Jewish people have had no place to offer sacrifices to God thus they seek atonement each year through fasting and good works.

To the Christians: The sacrifice of Yeshua Jesus on the cross is our atonement and the atonement for all who surrender to Him as Lord and Savior. I John 1:9 says: "If we confess our sins, He is faithful and righteous to forgive us our sins and to cleanse us from all unrighteousness".

The Temple Sacrifices on Yom Kippur

Yom Kippur was the one day of the year when the High Priest could enter into the Holy of Holies in the Temple in Jerusalem. He would take off his ornate priestly robes and put on a simple white linen tunic, a linen sash, linen undergarments, and turban which were holy garments – Leviticus 16:3-5. After performing the required animal sacrifices to God, the High Priest would sprinkle the blood from the sacrificed animals on the Mercy Seat. Imagine the look of his white garments covered in blood after he had slaughtered the animals for sacrifice! When the garments were stained at the point that the blood could not be washed out, they were cut into strips and used as wicks in the temple menorah, or in Yeshua Jesus' case, as swaddling cloths!

During the time of the Temple in Jerusalem, during the holiest day of the Hebrew year, Aaron would select two identical goats without a spot or blemish. He would then cast lots for the two goats, one lot for the Lord and the other lot for the scapegoat. The purpose of both of these goats was to atone for the sins of the people. The one that drew the lot for the Lord would be sacrificed completely on the altar as a sin offering to the Lord. On the other goat, called the Azazel in Hebrew, was placed the sins of the people. Aaron would tie a red sash around its horns and lay his hands on its head to make atonement on it by confessing the sins of the people. The Azazel would then be led out of the city by another priest and thrown over a cliff in the wilderness so it would die. The people did not want to simply release the goat into the wilderness for fear it would return to the city carrying their sins with it.

At the same time, a strip of red sash was placed on the Temple door on Yom Kippur. After the scapegoat had died, the red sash on the Temple door would miraculously turn white. This showed the people that their sacrifice had been accepted by the Lord and that their sins had been forgiven. After Yeshua died in 33 AD and for almost forty years until the Temple was destroyed by the Romans in 70 AD, the sash on the horns of the scapegoat and the sash on the temple door never turned white again. Additionally, after Yeshua' death, the western most light on the Temple menorah would not burn. The seventy foot tall Temple doors normally took twenty men to close, due to their weight, would open by themselves. Josephus recorded that the temple doors were of brass and were bolted and fastened into the floor. The fact that the doors opened freely without assistance meant that desolation was coming upon the Jewish people.

What is the Azazel?

Leviticus 16:10 says: "But the goat on which the lot for the Azazel fell shall be presented alive before the Lord, to make atonement upon it, to send it into the wilderness as the scapegoat".

There is no exact translation for the Hebrew word Azazel but it is often transliterated as scapegoat. Some researchers thought the word was for a specific place where the scapegoat was taken to die since the Gemara interprets the word as "hardest of the mountain", but since the Hebrews were a nomadic people this idea is probably not the case. It is more likely that they would want to have a place near their current location in which to kill the scapegoat on Yom Kippur. Therefore the name Azazel may refer to several different locations where sacrifices were performed. Some locations may be close to Shiloh and others may have been closer to Jerusalem. Differing locations could have been used at different times thorough out the history of Israel. Therefore, the word "Azazel" may simply be a general term used to describe a mountain top in the wilderness where the ceremony was performed on Yom Kippur.

In Medieval times, the Azaz'el was thought to have something to do with a demon. In more contemporary times the Azaz'el is connected with hell. This idea of taking the goat that was carrying the sins of the people to a desolate place from which there was no return does describe hell, the abode of demons. The purpose of the Azaz'el then was to serve the function of a substitionary death from which there was not return. So when we speak of the Azaz'el or use the term scapegoat, the punishment it received was a substitute for something it did not do, but it is made to suffer as an atonement for the sins of others.

This leads us to the sacrifice of Yeshua. Yeshua Jesus received cruel and undeserved punishment at the hand of Pontius Pilate and the Roman soldiers even though He was innocent of any wrongdoing. He was nailed to the pole/cross to suffer a horrible death. By so doing, He became the atonement for our sins, just like the Azaz'el. In addition, we know that the stained garments of the priests were cut into strips for wicks when they were too blood stained to use. Yeshua Jesus, Our High Priest, was probably wrapped in strips from the priestly garments after His birth! The scripture tells us that Elizabeth was Mary's [Miriam] cousin and that Elizabeth was married to Zechariah who was a Temple priest. She would have had access to the old, blood stained priestly garments. Thus the swaddling cloths placed on Yeshua Jesus at His birth where likely blood stained priestly garments. They represented His priesthood and His blood sacrifice for the sins of the world.

Why were goats used?

The goats represented deception and sin. Jacob deceived Isaac by putting goat skins on his arms so he would receive Esau's blessings. Joseph's brothers put goat blood on Joseph's coat and took it to their father as proof of Joseph's death. It was a lie. In truth, they sold Joseph as a slave to the Ishmaelites for twenty skekels of silver – Genesis 37:27-28.

Note: Joseph's coat was probably made of colors of goat hair. It's interesting that Joseph's coat was striped, the Holocaust prisoners wore striped clothing, and Yeshua Jesus was striped by a Roman soldier's whip.

Bloodless Sacrifices

Some rabbis refer to Daniel's Prayer to justify the lack of animal blood sacrifices. They believe the Bible provides atonement without the spilling of blood. They ignore the fact that the Bible says "life is in the blood", and it is blood that atones for the soul. Sam Nadler wrote that "By rejecting the blood atonement the rabbis both demean the holiness of God and minimize the offensiveness of sin". God set up the sacrificial system. The total consumption of the burnt offering is a picture that everything a man has belongs to God. The shedding of the blood of an innocent animal is meant to show us how serious our sins are toward a Holy God, and the fact that sin kills. God does not accept a bloodless sacrifice. If so, Yeshua would not have had to die for our sins on the cross. While He was in the Garden of Gethsemane He asked the Father to remove this cup from Him if there was another way, but there wasn't, and He surrendered to His father's will and shed His blood so others could be saved from hell and the grave.

Why was the blood sacrifice of Yeshua necessary?

1. The Scripture says "the life of all flesh is in the blood" - Leviticus 17:14. So God's Son came to earth to shed His blood so that all who believes in Him will have eternal life.
2. The blood sacrifice of Yeshua Jesus gives forgiveness to all who surrender to Him.
3. Believers in Yeshua Jesus have been purchased and redeemed by His blood sacrifice.
4. The blood of Yeshua Jesus cleanses believers from all their sin. It is as if one's sins never happened.
5. The blood justifies believers before the Father.
6. "It is impossible for the blood of bulls and of goats to take away sins" –Hebrews 10:4 7. Neither prayer nor good deeds will substitute for blood of Yeshua Jesus.

How the Jewish People Celebrate Yom Kippur Today

Since Yom Kippur is the most holy day of the Jewish year, religious Jews fast, pray, and seek forgiveness for their sins through good works since there is no longer a temple in which to offer an animal sacrifice for atonement. They hope that during Yom Kippur their good works will outweigh the bad and their name will be written in the Book of Life for another year. It is essential that all Jews attend synagogue services during this time. All worshipers wear white apparel which represents righteousness. It is believed that on this day Satan has no power to oppose a plea to God for forgiveness. Revelation 12:10 says, "... for the accuser of our brethren is cast down, which accused them before our God day and night". This verse supports the fact that Satan can do nothing on the 356th day which is Yom Kippur. After the service, the shofar is blown, and God's judgment is sealed for another year.

A Yom Kippur Service at El Shaddai Ministries – 2015 and 2016

With a heart full of excitement, my husband and I drove nine hours from our home in Montana to Tacoma, Washington. We had seen a Yom Kippur service on-line but had never attended one in person. We had purchased our white apparel weeks in advance and felt prepared. We arrived at our hotel in Tacoma with three hours to spare so we had time to unpack our clothing and freshen up before the service began. We arrived at the church forty-five minutes ahead of time and were surprised to see that the parking lot was already ¾ full of cars. We walked into the church full of anticipation. It felt like we were being embraced and welcomed by the Holy Spirit. Everyone we saw was dressed in white, just like the temple priests of old as they went into the Holy of Holies to sacrifice for the nation. A beautiful golden replica of the Ark of the Covenant sat in front of the altar. It was bathed in red light. The red light represented Yeshua Jesus' blood on the Mercy Seat. To the left side of it was a hundred year old Torah scroll. On the two side walls were screens displaying a box which contained the words, "God's Torah is a Hidden Treasure of Light and Life". The service started with the

"Shema" followed by the lighting of the menorah and the blowing of the shofar. The flag of Israel and a flag with a picture of the Lion of Judah was brought into the sanctuary and given places of honor in front of the altar and beside the Ark of the Covenant. When the service began we sang songs of praise to our God and Savior. Two ladies, holding large golden flags shaped like wings of angels, stood on each side of the altar. There they bowed and sang "Holy, holy, holy" in front of the congregation. Everyone joined in the singing of "I am zealous over Zion" and "Like a canopy over me, You stretched out Your wings". Many of the congregants had their hands raised to the Lord as they sang. On the right side of the stage, several ladies and young girls would wave white flags in timing to the music. Two groups of dancers, one made up of men and one made up of women, danced the Hebrew circle dance on the left side front of the sanctuary, below the stage. Also on the left on the stage were the musicians. After the singing, Pastor Mark Biltz gave an inspiring sermon on the meaning of Yom Kippur and how Yeshua Jesus cleansed and redeemed those who follow Him. At the end of the service Pastor Mark pronounced the Aaronic Blessing over the congregation in Hebrew and English. Then, all too quickly, the service was over. We left the sanctuary with joy in our hearts and a desire to return again to be part of this glorious service of praise and worship.

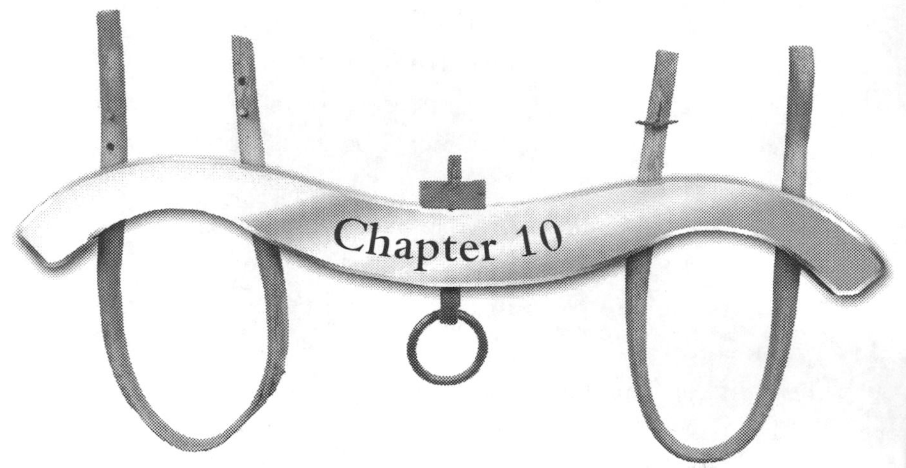

The Feast of Sukkot/Tabernacles

The Feast of Sukkot is most commonly known as the Feast of Tabernacles. Sukkot is the Hebrew word meaning "booths". In ancient times the Feast of Sukkot was a form of harvest festival but was not a unified celebration. It is held on the fifteenth of Tishri [September-October] and is often called the Feast of Thanksgiving and the Feast of Rejoicing. [The American Thanksgiving comes from this feast]. It is the third Fall feast that will be fulfilled at the Second Coming of Yeshua Jesus, and the seventh feast of the year. It takes place when the grapes, figs, and olives have been harvested, and is held at the beginning of the rain and new winter planting season. It is one of three pilgrimage feasts, Passover, Pentecost, and Tabernacle, where attendance in Jerusalem is mandatory for Jewish males and where they "appear before the Lord" – Deuteronomy 16:16. It also points to eternity when people from every nation and tribe and tongue will stand before the throne and before the Lamb...with palm branches in their hands; and crying out with loud voices declaring, "Salvation to our God who sits on the throne, and to the Lamb" – Revelation 7:9. Zechariah 14:16-17 warns what will happen during the Millennial Reign of Messiah to those people groups who do not attend the Feast of Tabernacles [Booths]: "Then it will come about that any one who are left of all the nations that went against Jerusalem will go up from year to year to worship the King, the Lord of Hosts,

and to celebrate the Feast of Booths [Tabernacles]. And it will be that whichever of the families of the earth does not go up to Jerusalem to worship the King, the Lord of hosts, there will be no rain on them". Why did God choose this type of punishment? Because without rain, neither crops nor people can survive.

This feast is symbolic of the long awaited Messianic Kingdom on earth! It is a time of worship when Yeshua Jesus will rule as King and Lord over all, and the Sabbath rest will be restored and enjoyed throughout eternity.

The Feast of Tabernacles has many other names. It is called the Feast of Booths, the Feast of Nations, the Feast of Rejoicing, the Feast of Praising, the Feast of the Lulav, the Feast of Rain, the Feast of Ingathering, and the Feast of Homecoming. It takes place at the end of the harvest season. It runs from the fifteenth of Tishri to the twenty-first of Tishri [usually beginning at the end of September or in early October on the Julian calendar].

To the Jews: This feast is celebrated at the end of the harvest season when the grapes, olives, and figs are harvested. The people offer thanks to God for His blessings and provision. Devout Jews build a temporary dwelling place called a sukkah, hut, or booth. This reminds them of their frailness, of their dependence upon God, and of the wandering of their ancestors through the desert from Egypt to the Promised Land. They also pray for rain for the coming winter planting of crops.

To the Christians: This feast speaks of the Millennial Reign when Yeshua Jesus, the Messiah will rule the earth as King of Kings, and Lord of Lords. It is a joyful time of worship and praise to God. It represents His completed work in the lives of the redeemed who have surrendered to Him as their Lord and Savior.

Leviticus 23: 39-43 says: "On exactly the fifteenth day of the seventh month, when you have gathered in the crops of the land, you shall celebrate the feast of the Lord for seven days, with a rest on the first day and a rest on the eighth day. Now on the first day you shall take for yourselves the foliage of beautiful trees, palm branches, and boughs of leafy trees and willows of the brook, and you shall rejoice before the Lord your God for seven days. You shall thus celebrate it as a feast to the Lord for seven days in the year. It shall be a perpetual statute throughout your

generations; you shall celebrate it in the seventh month. You shall live in booths for seven days; all the native-born in Israel shall live in booths, so that your generations may know that I had the sons of Israel live in booths when I brought them out of Egypt. I am the Lord your God".

The Sukkah

After Yom Kippur, devout Jews continue to build a sukkah for the Feast of Tabernacles. It is a small, portable hut which is also called a booth. They sleep and eat their meals during the seven days of the feast in the sukkah which is built near their house. In the ancient past the sukkah was built from the four species mentioned in Leviticus 23:40. It consisted of walls of plaited branches and thatched roofs. Today, like then, it must be made from something that grew out of the ground and are substantial. Wooden materials like lattice, two-by-four boards, sticks and corn stalks can be used, in addition to fabrics and leafy branches of trees. It must be built so it will not blow away in the wind. The roof is open enough that when inside, one can look up into the sky and see the stars and feel the evening breeze; but not so open that the rain or sun comes in.

The description of how to build a sukkah is found in Leviticus 23:39-42. Many of these huts are beautifully decorated on the inside with hanging flowers, fruits, and greenery, especially in the Samaritan culture in the West Bank of Israel.

The sukkah has three significant meanings: First, it is to remind the Jews of how their ancestors had lived in temporary, portable huts, while on their way through the desert to the Promised Land. Second, the sukkah is symbolic of David's throne, and that of Messiah, when the world is filled with blessings and He is king over all the earth. Third, the sukkah represents the redeemed of the Lord dwelling with God and God dwelling with them. Many Christians believe that the Marriage Supper of the Lamb will take place in a big sukkah on the Feast of Tabernacles.

Note: There was a prophecy given to Prime Minister Nethanyahu of Israel the second time he took office. It warned him not to exchange land for peace. He had not listened to a warning the first time he was Prime Minister and as a result he was removed. The second time he was warned, he listened. He was also told during the second prophecy he was given that he would see the tabernacle of David. This could mean that the building of the foundation of the Temple will start this year. This prophecy indicates that the return of Messiah is close at hand.

The Lulav

A lulav is made up of the four species of plants mentioned in the Torah in Leviticus 23:40. They are the palm, myrtle, and willow branches which are bound together with a golden thread and held in the right hand. They are carried around the altar one time each day for the first six days, and seven times on the seventh day. A citrus fruit called an etrog is also carried. Originally the lulav was only to be used for seven days in the Temple in Jerusalem. After the temple was destroyed in 70 AD, the lulav could be used anywhere for seven day, in memory of the Temple. It is to be held in the following fashion. First, The etrog is held in the left hand with its spine toward the user, and its tip pointed down. The etrog is a yellow-colored, lemon-like fruit from the citron tree that symbolizes the fruit of the Promised Land. The user brings his or her two hands together so that the etrog touches the lulav bundle. Then a Hebrew prayer of thanks called the Shehekeyanu, which means "He supports us", is recited. After the blessing, the etrog is turned right side up and shaken gently with the four species three times toward each of the four directions, north, south, east, and west, plus up and down. These directions all illustrate that no matter where one goes to escape from God, God is already there; from the highest heaven to the deepest hell.

During the time of the second Temple, the willow branches were cut on the eve of the Sabbath and placed in golden basins filled with water to keep them fresh. If the first day of the Feast of Tabernacles fell on the Sabbath, people would bring their lulavim [plural form of lulav] to the Temple Mount on Friday where all the lulavim would be arranged in rows on the benches that surrounded the Temple Mount. The next day the people would arrive early to pick up their lulav which were thrown before them by the sexton. The people were instructed if anyone touched their lulav, it should be considered a gift to that person. This did not bode well. When people reached for their lulav, and someone else caught it, anger would flare and fights would break out. To avoid this type of negative behavior on the part of the people, the High Court ruled that each person should bless their lulav in their own house rather than bringing it to the Temple Mount.

There were times when the Feast of Tabernacles fell on a week day rather than on the Sabbath. In this case, the people would set their willow branches on the sides of the altar, so the tops bent over the altar. This formed a beautiful type of canopy over the altar.

Psalm 139:7-12 says, "Where can I go from Your Spirit? Or where can I flee from Your presence? If I ascend to heaven, You are there; If I make my bed in Sheol, behold, You are there. If I take the winds of the dawn, if I dwell in the remotest part of the sea, even there Your hand will lead me, and Your right hand will lay hold of me. If I say, 'Surely the darkness will overwhelm me, and the light around me will be night', even the darkness is not dark to You, and the night is as bright as the day. Darkness and light are alike to You".

During the Millennial Reign, the Lord Yeshua Jesus will rule and be worshiped by all peoples, from every nation on the earth during the Feast of Tabernacles.

There are several Jewish explanations for the importance of the lulav that are held by the Jewish people. The first explanation is that the four species of plants represent the desire by devout Jews for all four types of Jews to be united in service to God. First, the ripe green closed palm frond of the lulav has taste but no smell. It symbolizes those who study Torah but do not possess good deeds. Second, the myrtle (hadassah) has a pleasant smell but no taste. This symbolizes those who perform good deeds but do not study Torah. Third, the willow has neither taste nor smell. This symbolizes those who neither study the Torah nor perform good deeds. Fourth, the etrog has both a good taste and a good smell. It symbolizes those who both study the Torah and perform good deeds.

A second possibility is that the four species represent the human body. The spine of the body is represented by the palm, the eye is represented by the myrtle, the mouth is represented by the willow, and the heart is represented by the etrog. By binding them together, the Jews show their desire to consecrate their entire being to God's service.

A third explanation for the four species is that the three branches and the etrog represent geographical locations the Jewish people traveled on their way to the land of promise; the valleys where palm trees grow and provide shade from the heat of the sun, the mountains where the sweet myrtle flowers bloom, the brooks with cool flowing water to quench one's thirst and the etrog, a citrus fruit, which represents the abundant provisions of the Promise land. The children of Israel were led by God through each of these four types of terrain after they left Egypt This assures us that no matter where our journey may take us in this life, God in His faithfulness is always with us, ready to bless us, and is an ever present help as we His children serve Him.

Christian Meaning of the Lulav

For the born-again Christian, the lulav represents several significant meanings. The first meaning of the lulav is: the palm branch is a symbol of peace, victory, and the triumphal entry of Messiah into Jerusalem on Palm Sunday. Second, the myrtle is a symbol of Messiah's love for all people. Third, the willow branch is a symbol of Messiah's weeping over those who refuse to accept Him as Lord and Savior.

Pastor Mark Biltz suggests that the palm branch represents God's righteousness and power to save. The myrtle represents praise and rejoicing. The willow represents Yeshua's humility, the suffering servant. The etrog represents the Lord's beauty and that He is a branch bearing fruit.

Michael Norten suggests that the palm branches are a reminder to the Jewish people of the valleys and plains. The bough of trees is a reminder of bushes on the mountains. The willows remind them of the brooks. The etrog reminds them of the fruits of the land God has given to them.

Sam Nadler suggests that the four species represent Messiah's power to save and His righteousness, praise and rejoicing; Christ's humility and suffering; and the Lord's beauty.

Perry Stone believes that each tree represents four experiences in life. The palm branch represents victory over the beast's kingdom. The myrtle branch is tied to the palm representing rest on the Sabbath. The willow branch is a symbol of sorrow and weeping. The etrog [citron] represents times of bitterness.

The Year-End Feast and Celebration in the Temple

Sukkot was the final feast of the Jewish year. This took place after the Fall harvest. Approximately two million people were present at this feast in Jerusalem. They were commanded by the Lord to be joyful during the seven days of Sukkot. Each day the priest would wave the branches of the lulav in every directions – north, south, east, west, up and down in the Temple to show that God is omnipresent and rules over everything in His creation.

In the ancient days before Chanukah, this feast was called the "Festival of Light" as thousands of pilgrims came to Jerusalem carrying lighted torches. The temple hoisted four 75 feet tall golden lamps. These stood in the Court of the Women. Each lamp had four golden bowls sitting on the top of it. The wicks used in the lamps were made from old, stained priestly garments. Young priests-in-training would climb up a ladder and fill the golden bowls with pure olive oil from seven gallon buckets. Once filled, they would light the golden lamps. It was said because the Temple sat on a hill [the Temple Mount] above the city of Jerusalem, the light from the lamps was so bright that one could see the glow of them in every courtyard in Jerusalem. The light produced by these lamps represented the Shekinah glory of God that filled His Temple as the Jews recognized God as the true light.

Tall, elevated balconies were constructed which enabled the righteous women, as they sang, to watch the men of the Sanhedrin as they danced and carried torches around the temple. The Levites, standing on the fifteenth step that descended from the Court of Israel to the Women's Court, played music from harps, trumpets, lyres, and various other musical instruments. Two priests blew silver trumpets from the top of the stairs at the great gate of the Court.

During the seven days of the feast, seventy bulls were sacrificed at dawn; one for each of the seventy nations in the world at the time of the Temple. After the animal sacrifices, the priests engaged in prayer. The eighth day was a Sabbath day. It is called Shemini Atzeret. On that day only one bull was sacrificed. This bull was for Israel.

The Water Libation Ceremony

The Water Libation Ceremony was the most jubilant ceremony of the Feast of Tabernacles/Sukkot during the time of the second temple period. Its approach was much anticipated throughout the harvest season by men, women, and children. When it came, everyone joyfully participated. While the feast lasted all night for seven nights, the Water Libation Ceremony took place on the seventh night. It has been said that "whoever has not seen the celebration of the water libation has never experienced the feeling of true joy".

First, the priests were divided into three groups. The first group was responsible for slaying all the animals that would be sacrificed. The second group of priests, headed up by the High Priest, would go out through the Water Gate to the pool of Siloam to get the "living water". Living water is spring fed water or flowing or running water that represents the Lord. The third group went out the Eastern Gate and proceeded to the Motzah Valley [the Kidron Valley] to cut 20 – 25 feet long willow branches.

For six days the High Priest would walk around the altar once singing Psalm 118:25. which says: "O Lord, do save, we beseech You; O Lord, we beseech You, do send prosperity!" Seventy animals for the seventy nations of the world would be sacrificed. The people in the Temple courtyard would pray for God's blessings of rain for the coming planting season.

At dawn on the seventh day, a group of priests, headed by the High Priest, went out through the Water Gate and descended to the pool of Siloam, located at the foot of the walls of the City of David in Jerusalem. The whole road leading to the Temple was lined with thousands of pilgrims waving lulavs and singing Hoshiaynu [hosanna] meaning "save us now". Once at the pool, the High Priest filled a golden pitcher full of the water known as the "living water". His assistant held a silver bowl containing wine. The High Priest accompanying other groups of priests ascended once more to the Temple and returned through the Eastern gate as multitudes of pilgrims lined the road to join in the celebration. At a certain signal, the priests with the willow branches would march with precision back up to the Temple waving the willow branches back and forth. As they did this, the movement of the willow branches created a swishing sound like a "rushing wind". [Wind in Hebrew is Ruach]. When each of the three separate parties reached their designated gates upon return, a shofar was blown, once for each group. Then a flute player, called "the pierced one", would blow the call for both the wind and water to enter the Temple as he led the procession of priests. Both the wind and the water represent the Holy Spirit coming upon Jerusalem.

First, the priests carrying the willow branches made their way to the altar. They stood shoulder to shoulder. There were many lines of priests who stood in rows of 25-30 feet behind each other per row, and moved their feet in unison as they swished the willow branches. Then they circled the altar seven times forming a canopy over the altar.

Second, the priests who were slaughtering the animals for sacrifice now approached the altar. They laid the sacrifices on the fire on the altar.

Third, the High Priest and his assistant ascended to the altar, and all the people of Israel were gathered into the courts around them. All the children of Israel assembled there were singing: "With joy we will draw water out of the well of salvation" [Yeshua] – Pastor Biltz. The High Priest then brings the golden pitcher up to the bronze altar. A silver cup containing wine sat at a corner by the horns of the altar. Two bowls were built into the altar. The High Priest pours the wine from the silver pitcher into the cup of "living water". The pitcher containing the mixture of wine and "living water" was then poured out over the altar and into the two bowls where it would flow down a conduit to the Kidron Brook, located across from the Eastern wall. As the water and wine mixture was poured out, the priests with the willow branches started laying the willow against the altar to form a sukkah. The sukkah created a picture of God's covering.

Hoshana Raba

The seventh day is called Hoshana Raba. This means "The Great Hosanna and The Great Salvation". The High Priest, accompanied by the other priests, would walk around the altar seven times as the crowds of people chanted "Hoshana prayers" - "we will gather water from the well of salvation" [Yeshua] from Isaiah 12:3 and shout "Hosanna" which means "Save us now". Yeshua' brothers kept telling Him to tell the people who He is at this point but Yeshua Jesus was silent and waited until the right time. At the same time, the willows were being beaten. With each circular progression, the cry of the crowds for the provision of water for their crops and salvation, grew louder and louder until they reached a crescendo. It was here that Yeshua cried out, ... "If anyone is thirsty, let him come to Me and drink. He who believes in Me, as the Scripture said, 'From his innermost being will flow rivers of living water'" But this He spoke of the Spirit, whom those who believed in Him were to receive; for the spirit was not yet given, because Jesus was not yet glorified" – John 7:37-39. By saying this, Yeshua Jesus was declaring that He is the Messiah. As a result of His words, "a division occurred in the crowd"; some thought He was a Prophet while others thought that he was the Messiah; some said He had a demon and others wanted to seize Him – John 8, still no one touched Him for fear of the Jewish leaders, the words He had spoken, and the fact that it was not yet His time.

The Talmud gives a very informative description of a priest's description of the Water Libation ceremony. It was incredibly tiring since they got very little sleep for the seven days of the feast. Prayers and daily offerings to the Lord were performed continuously, morning, noon and night. This process was repeated for seven days and nights. In addition to this, the celebration of the Festival of the Water Libation was held. It lasted an entire night, and when completed, the priests would have to start the entire process over again.

The ceremony had two major meanings. First, the water represented the coming of Messiah and His kingdom in which the Holy Spirit of God will be poured out on them, as the prophets had predicted. Indeed this happened during Pentecost and continues to happen today on believers in Yeshua. Second, the ceremony was connected to the prayers of the people in which they asked God for the blessings of rainfall on the earth and on its produce during the coming year.

The Eighth Day

The eighth day is the day following the feast, a Sabbath, a day of rest. It is described in Numbers 29:35-36. It says: "On the eighth day you shall have a solemn assembly; you shall do no laborious work. But you shall present a burnt offering, an offering by fire, as a soothing aroma to the Lord: one bull, ...".

The eighth day that followed the seven days of the Feast of Tabernacles was a festival called Shemini Atzeret. It includes Simchat Torah, the rejoicing of the Torah. Atzeret in Hebrew means "to hold back or stop". The number eight is symbolic of "new beginnings". For seven days the Israelites had brought offerings before the Lord and sacrificed seventy bulls for the seventy nations, but on the eighth day only one bull and one ram was sacrificed. That bull and ram was sacrificed for Israel only – Numbers 29:36. It is a sad note that the nations Israel was blessing by the sacrifices, were the very nations that hated Israel! Had those nations only known what Israel was doing on their behalf things could have changed for the better between them and Israel. But Satan had another plan. He wanted to destroy Israel so he could stop the birth of the Savior/Messiah that would come from them. He knew if the Messiah came, his time to rule the earth would be short and his end near.

Another belief about the eighth day is that since it is the last day appointed by God, it refers to eternity. In a sense, when the redeemed turn their focus away from their problems and focus on the Word of the Lord, they are experiencing the joys of eternity in present time.

Simchat Torah is the annual celebration which honors the final reading of the Torah found in Deuteronomy 34. After this reading, devout Jews would return back to Genesis 1 and begin reading the Torah from the beginning again. The celebration occurs at the end of the Feast of Tabernacles on the twenty-fourth day of Tishri, the eighth day. At the end of the eighth day the 75 foot high candles in the Court of the Women were extinguished.

Yeshua Jesus at the Feast of Tabernacles in the Future

The Feast of Tabernacles or Sukkot had a special meaning to Yeshua Jesus who came to this feast twice. The first time He came was on the fourth day. The number four represents Creation and is God's signature of the world. The second time He came was on the seventh day. The number seven represents divine completeness and the union of earth with heaven. Those two days Messiah chose also represented the fact that He came to earth the first time 2,000 years ago and after He returns at His Second Coming, the Millennial Reign will begin on the 7,000th year after Creation. When He came the first time, He died to redeem fallen humanity. As He hung on the pole/cross, His blood dripped from the crown of thorns that pierced His head, from His pierced side where the Roman soldier had stabbed Him with his spear, and from His pierced extremities with which He was nailed to the pole/cross. He is truly the "pierced one" mentioned in Zechariah 12:10. Isaiah 53:5 describes His suffering and agony on our behalf. It says: "But He was pierced through for our transgressions, He was crushed for our iniquities; the chastening for our well-being fell upon Him, and by His scourging we are healed".

When He comes the second time, He is coming as King of Kings and Lord of Lords over all the earth. He will set up His kingdom on earth for 1,000 years prior to the Sabbath rest in heaven. His rule on earth is known as the Millennial Reign. During Messiah's rule, the Sabbath will be reinstated, as will the sacrifices and festivals. These memorials will be held forever to commemorate Messiah's sacrifice for mankind. Everyone will be required to attend the Feast of Tabernacles in Jerusalem, along with Passover and Pentecost. If they refuse, as mentioned earlier, their land will receive no rain and they will not survive.

When Yeshua Jesus reigns, Sukkot will be called the "Feast of the Kingdom". This feast ushers in the Messianic Age. It is also the "Feast of Completion". It will be the end and completion of all things.

As Christians begin to understand and embrace the symbolism of the Feast of Tabernacles, a deeper meaning behind Yeshua' entry into Jerusalem on a donkey becomes clear. John 12:12-13 says: On the next day the large crowd who had come to the feast, when they heard that Jesus [Yeshua] was coming to Jerusalem, took the branches of the palm trees and went out to meet Him, and began to shout, "Hosanna! Blessed is He who comes in the name of the Lord, even the King of Israel." Perhaps they were recalling what Yeshua had said during the Feast of Tabernacles. Revelation 7:9 tells us that, "a multitude from the Tribulation were before the Lamb, clothed in white robes, and palm branches were in their hands". The palm branches were a symbol of their victory over Satan.

When was Yeshua Jesus Born – At Passover, in Summer, or during Sukkot?

There is a debate about the time of Yeshua's birth. All agree that He was born in Bethlehem Ephrathah – Micah 5:2. Are those two names significant? The answer is yes! In Hebrew the word for bread is lechem. Bethlehem means the House of Lechem or Bread. What does Ephrathah stand for? It comes from the Hebrew word peree which means the fruit of the vine [wine]. So the place of Yeshua's birth, Bethlehem Ephrathah means bread and wine. Thus those two Hebrew words connect together His death with the place of His birth. Bread and wine are the two elements Yeshua Jesus introduced to His disciples just prior to His death following their Seder meal on Passover. They represent His body and His blood. When believers participate in the Lord's Supper or Communion, they are remembering Yeshua's body and blood that was sacrificed for our redemption..

Some scholars believe He was born in the Spring on Passover – March 20, 06 AD while other scholars say He was born on Sukkot/ Tabernacles in the Fall. While the scripture doesn't give us a specific date, it does give us two hints that have helped scholars identify two possible years for His birth. They have defined His birth as occurring between the years 04 AD and 06 AD. How did they arrive at those years? First, there was a decree that went out from Caesar Augustus that ordered a census be taken of everyone that inhabited earth ... each to his own city – Luke 2:1-3. He needed a census in order to collect more taxes from the people because of his lavish lifestyle. Second, there were shepherds staying out in their fields to watch their sheep at night - Luke 2:8. The flocks were kept in the stables during the winter months because of the cold weather. They were released to the outdoors from the week before Passover until mid-November, using our calendar. Therefore the night time temperatures had to be warm enough for the shepherds and their flocks to remain outdoors all night. Based on this, one can eliminate the winter months as a time of Yeshua's birth. New life in the land of Israel starts in the Spring of the year when the weather begins to warm up. Since Yeshua Jesus is the lamb of God, he was likely born around Passover, during the lambing season in Spring. Thus we can eliminate a winter birth. That leaves us with Spring, Summer, or Fall as possible birth dates.

1. Lets consider a Spring birthdate as a possibility. This is the time of the religious new year for the Jews. God gave them Nisan 1 as their new year to separate them from the other nations. It is the only date He gave them to mark a new beginning. It is a time when the sheep are in the fields, lambs were being born, and winter was past. It is a time of new birth in all of nature; the trees bud, the flowers bloom and the fields are planted. Yeshua, the Lamb of God could have been born on Nisan 1 which means "the beginning". If so, Joseph, his earthly father, could have made it to Jerusalem from Bethlehem in time for the celebration of Passover on Nisan 14 as commanded by God. In addition, His birth fits the story of the Magi who sought the baby Messiah because of the convergence of three planets: Jupiter, Saturn, and Mars which formed the Bethlehem star. Thus He could have been born on March 20, 06 as the Passover Lamb.

It was recorded that Yeshua was born in a stable [The Tower of Eder] and wrapped in swaddling cloths from stained priestly garments. Special temple priests would wrap new born lambs in strips of stained priestly garments to keep them from getting blemished. These lambs were used in temple sacrifices and kept, as many believe, in the Tower of Eder. Yeshua is our High Priest.

2. Lets consider a Summer birthdate. According to some writers, Yeshua was born on a Sunday, August 21, 07 AD, at 12:00 p.m. This date was tabulated based on the Julian and Gregorian calendars. While these calendars differed in leap years, one date that was constant in both calendars, August 21, 07 AD. That was also the date when there was a conjunction of Jupiter and Saturn which could explain the star the shepherds saw over Bethlehem the night Yeshua was born. This date is unlikely however for two reasons. First, this date was when Noah released the black raven after the flood. Many people consider this bird to be a symbol of Satan. Second, it is unlikely as His birthdate because it does not connect with a feast day. Every significant event in Yeshua's life occurred on a feast date.

3. Lets consider a Fall birthdate. The book of Luke tells us that Mary went quickly to see her cousin Elizabeth after meeting with the angel

who told her the Holy Spirit would come upon her and she would be impregnated with the son of God. Some people believe this occurred on the Feast of Chanukah in early December since Yeshua is the light of the world and Chanukah was also known as the Festival of Light. If this date is correct, Yeshua Jesus would have been born during the Feast of Tabernacles/Sukkot at the end of September or early October. The shepherds would still in the fields at this time watching over their sheep, but they wouldn't be baby lambs at this time. Joseph would be breaking the Law if he had stayed in Bethlehem for Yeshua's birth since all men were required to be in Jerusalem for Sukkot. It was one of the three pilgrimage feasts where attendance was mandatory. Elizabeth would have had access to old blood-stained priestly garments since Zacharias was a temple priest, so Mary would have had access to them. There was also the conjunction of three planets: Jupiter, Saturn and Mars. This could explain the star the shepherds saw in the sky over Bethlehem the night Yeshua was born. The problem with this date is that the Feast of Sukkot/ Tabernacles was the last feast of the harvest year.

One point all scholars do agree upon is that Yeshua Jesus was NOT born on December 25th, the date of the winter solstice. That date was chosen to appeal to pagans with the hope that they would be converted and brought into the church.

Was Yeshua Jesus born in a stable, a tower, or a house?

Several researchers have written that Yeshua Jesus was probably born in the Tower of Migdal Eder which literally means the "Tower of Eder". This tower is the same one referred to as "the tower of the flock" in Micah 4:8 and was first mentioned in Genesis 35:21. It is one of three possible locations that was sanctified and believed to be used to house newborn lambs for temple use. It was located about six miles from Jerusalem, near the small town of Bethlehem. It was in the area mentioned in Micah 5:2 which says: "But as for you, Bethlehem Ephrathah, too little to be among the clans of Judah, from you One will go forth for Me to be ruler in Israel. His goings forth are from long ago, from the days of eternity". It has also been said by the Sages that animals that were found and kept in the fields near Migdal Eder were also declared holy and used as sacrificial animals in the temple.

The Tower of Migdal Eder has been described by several writers as a two story tower from which special shepherds from the temple watched over the new born lambs. After the lambs were born they were inspected and if perfect were placed in the lower room of the tower. There the little lambs where wrapped in cloths from old, blood stained priestly garments to keep them from being blemished or harmed. The shepherds would also watch over their other animals from the upper story of the tower. These were the animals that were raised to be sacrificed in the Temple.

The Scripture tells us that Yeshua was wrapped in swaddling cloths and was laid in a manger. What a perfect picture of His priesthood on earth! The word manger can be translated "stall" as in Luke 13:15 or be referred to as any holding place for animals. It is most likely that it was in these shepherds' fields that the angels proclaimed the Good News of Yeshua's birth!

Some students of the Scriptures believe that Yeshua Jesus was born in a house since Joseph had many relatives living in Bethlehem. They believe that Mary and Joseph were comfortably housed up to several months prior to Yeshua's birth by Joseph's relatives. The Bible does not indicate that this is the case since Yeshua Jesus was placed in a manger after His birth. Another fact to consider is that Mary and Joseph were very poor. God provided for His Son's earthly family by sending the Magi with gifts. This explains why the arrival of the Magi to Jerusalem, a journey which likely took up to twenty-four months, upset Herod who feared for the loss of his position as king. Since Mary, Joseph and Yeshua were no longer in Bethlehem at that time, it is probable that they had returned home to Nazareth after Yeshua Jesus was born and that Yeshua Jesus was a toddler at the time the Magi came to Jerusalem. This explains why Herod ordered all males below the age of two years to be killed.

Regardless of the date, place, or feast of His birth, we need to focus on His resurrection. Without that, no human being could be redeemed. We are living in the Last Days. The Jewish people are back in their land after 2,000 years and the church is going back to its Jewish roots. Many Jews are eager to learn more about Yeshua or have already come to faith and saving knowledge of Him, their Messiah. Joel 2:28 says: It will come about ... that I will pour out My Spirit on all mankind. Your sons and daughter will prophecy, your old men will dream dreams, your young men will see visions. This is happening around the world today, even as the world is getting darker and darker spiritually. The Bible tells us after the redeemed joins the Lord in the air during the Rapture, that God's focus will once again turn to Israel. Even though the Word of God is being spread around the world today, sadly, only a small remnant in Israel has come to salvation. Most will have to endure the Tribulation Period and at that time will call out to their Messiah, Yeshua. Hosea 3:5 says: "Afterward the sons of Israel will return and seek the Lord their God and David their king; and they will come trembling to the Lord and to His goodness in the last days". Unfortunately many will be deceived and will surrender to the anti-Christ rather than their true Savior. They will learn the truth to late. After the Tribulation Period, at the end of the age, God will once dwell among His people like He did in the Garden of Eden and we will dwell in the house of the Lord forever. Amen!

What Do We Know About Yeshua Jesus

The following seven descriptors of Yeshua Jesus from the Scriptures were quoted from a sermon by Pastor Mark Biltz:

1. Firstborn of Mary	Matthew 1:23-25
2. First Begotten of God	Hebrews 1:6
3. Firstborn of every creature	Colossians 1:15
4. First Begotten of the dead	Revelation 1:5, Acts 26:23
5. Firstborn of many brethren	Romans 8:29
6. First Fruit of the resurrected ones	I Corinthians 15:14-23
7. Beginning of the creation of God	Revelation 3:14

My Journey to the Shepherds' Field

On our journey through the Holy Land, we spent one night in Bethlehem. The next morning we visited the Church of the Nativity and saw one of the suggested birthplace's of Yeshua Jesus. The site looked like a hole in the rock floor of the church, surrounded by a gold metal sunburst. Several feet above the sunburst, on each side and across the top of the rock, hung a dark blue velvet fabric curtain that formed a protective drapery. The site was believed to be the cave in which Yeshua Jesus was laid in a manger after His birth.

After lunch, we traveled a short distance to the Shepherds' Field. We entered a gate and walked down a well kept walkway lined with cedar trees. On the left side of the walkway, we passed by the stone ruins of the house believed to belong to Ruth and Boaz. Ruth 4:11 says, ... "may you achieve wealth in Ephrathah and become famous in Bethlehem". This verse refers to the same area mentioned as the birthplace of Yeshua and the probable location of Migdal Eder; the Tower of the Flocks; the place of the manger in which Yeshua was laid after His birth. Behind the church was a cave with a blackened ceiling. It is believed to be where the shepherds took turns eating their meals and sleeping during the night.

At the end of the walkway was a round, stone-shaped church. Over the front door were three archways. As we entered the church, we said an altar sitting toward the center of the room. Three wide, tall pictures depicting scenes of the nativity were on the wall behind the altar. The most striking feature, however, was the ceiling. It was covered with small, round openings that made the ceiling look as if the stars and light from heaven was shining through them into the room. As we stood with a group of other pilgrims, we spontaneously began to sing "Hark the Herald Angels Sing". The acoustics in the room were fantastic! It was like the worship and music was flowing up to heaven. Afterwards, everyone was silent for a few moments, quietly taking in a feeling of God's holy presence.

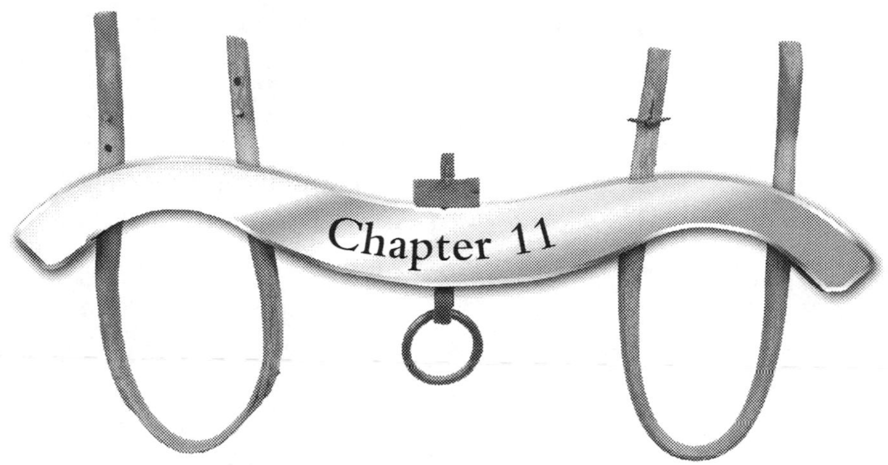

Chanukah: The Miracle of the Oil and The Re-Dedication of the Temple

Daniel 8:3-11 prophesizes the Chanukah events. He says: "Then I lifted up mine eyes, and looked, and behold, a ram which had two horns was standing in front of the canal. Now the two horns were long, but one was longer than the other, with the longer one coming up last. I saw the ram butting westward, northward, and southward, and no other beasts could stand before him nor was there anyone to rescue from his power, but he did as he pleased and magnified himself. While I was observing, behold, a male goat was coming from the west over the surface of the whole earth without touching the ground; and the goat had a conspicuous horn between his eyes. He came up to the ram with the two horns...and he was enraged at him...the male goat magnified himself exceedingly. But as soon as he was mighty, the large horn was broken, and in its place there came up four conspicuous horns ... out of one of them came forth a rather small horn which grew exceedingly great toward...the beautiful land...it even magnified itself...."

These verses in the book of Daniel are referring to Antiochus IV Epiphanes, a type of anti-Christ, whom the Jews defeated in order to reclaim their temple. The defeat by the Jews of the Greek army led by Antiochus IV Epiphanes and his sons led to the celebration of Chanukah on Kislev 25 each year. Their three year battle took place about 160 years before Yeshua Jesus was born. Antiochus IV set the pattern for the end-times anti-Christ.

Chanukah means "dedication". It derives its name from the consecration of the temple altar, not the entire temple, during the second temple period. While Chanukah is not one of the feasts of Moses, the miracle associated with Chanukah is one of the most memorable events in Jewish history and is a foreshadow of victory of good over evil at Messiah's return. Chanukah was established to be time of praise and thanksgiving to God. It is a story of light overcoming darkness and has sometimes been called a second Sukkot. It occurred during the 400 year period of time between the Old and New Testaments. It speaks of a temple originally built for God but became defiled. Its defilement occurred when Antiochus IV Epiphanes turned the temple of God into a temple for the pagan worship of Zeus. Antiochus IV saw himself as the manifestation of Zeus. As a result of his actions of defilement, the light in the temple menorah which represents the light of God's presence and the illumination of the Torah went out.

The history of Chanukah is recorded in the 1 Book of Maccabees. It records the Jewish defeat of the Greek army of Antiochus IV Epiphanes and their bravery and victory against tyranny. God helped the Jews win many battles over a three year period of time. As a result, they gained the right to practice their religion in freedom. They consisted of the few against the many and the good over evil. Deuteronomy 7:7 says, "The Lord did not set His love on you nor choose you because you were more in number than any of the peoples, for you were the fewest of all peoples, but because the Lord loved you ..." After God gave them victory, they cleansed their temple, lit the light in the Menorah, and re-dedicated the holy altar and temple to God.

The Background of Antiochus IV Epiphanes

Antiochus IV Epiphanes, whose name means "Divine" and "God Made Manifest", was ambitious and evil, a type of anti-Christ. He has been historically defined as the cruelest of the Seleucid kings. He ruled the Seleucid Empire from 175-164 BC. He saw himself as a god, a manifestation of Zeus; but the Jews called him "Epimanes", "The Mad One" because of his mad, absurd behaviors. He was determined to spread Hellenism throughout his empire no matter what the cost to the people. He was hedonistic, did not attempt to restrain his behaviors no matter how embarrassing to others, and was emotionally unstable. He lacked any form of modesty and would often dance naked at banquets with the entertainers he had hired. He was horrifically dishonest. He stole whatever he thought he needed. He desperately wanted a one world government and one world religion to unify his widely diverse ethnic and cultural empire. He cultivated pagan customs and introduced the barbaric gladiatorial games to the people in Syria. As if that were no enough, he ordered statues of himself to be erected in every temple of his empire and ordered the people to worship them. If a person refused, it meant certain death. Antiochus IV erected an idol of Zeus, "the abomination of desolation" spoken of by Daniel the prophet", in the holy temple. He sacrificed a pig on the holy altar to Zeus [near our month of December, in 168 BC] and poured its blood on the Torah. He forbade circumcision, Sabbath services, kosher foods, the celebration of the Feasts of the Lord and the new moons, and the study of the Torah. If a baby was circumcised, it was hung around its mother's neck, and both of them and those who participated in the circumcism were crucified and hung on the city walls. Many Jews gave in for sake of their lives but some refused to dishonor God's laws and Commandments. Therefore Antiochus IV had one problem that kept him from fulfilling his plan of Hellenizing his empire, the Jews and their refusal to obey his orders.

<u>Note:</u> The difference between Antiochus IV Epiphanes and Haman in the book of Esther is that Antiochus IV Epiphanes wanted the Jews to <u>assimilate</u> into his Hellenistic-style one world government and one world religion; to give up their faith and religious practices in their temple for the One True God. Haman wanted <u>annihilation</u>; death to all Jews.

How Antiochus IV Epiphanes Died

Antiochus IV Epiphanes went to steal treasures in the temple of Elymais, in Persia but the people resisted and he was forced to flee. As his empire began to disintegrate, he began to suffer more and more from debilitating stress and major depression. To make matters even worse, he contracted an unidentifiable disease from which he eventually lost the use of all of his extremities. He began to smell so foul that everyone avoided contact with him. He died in Persia in 163 BC, alone and deserted. Prior to his death he expressed regrets that he had needlessly oppressed the Jews and had defiled their holy temple.

The Historical Period of Chanukah

The history of Chanukah begins with the death of Alexander the Great, son of King Philip of Macedonia, during the second century. Because of his success as a military commander, Alexander's kingdom became one of the largest kingdoms in the medieval world. It stretched from Greece to northwestern India. When he suddenly died at the age of thirty-three without leaving an heir his kingdom was divided among his four generals, two of whom became strong; Ptolemy I who took Egypt and Seleucus I who ruled Syria. Israel became part of the Seleucid Empire and served as a buffer between Egypt and Syria. Before long, Antiochus of Asia Minor wanted to annex Babylonia and neighboring lands into his empire. As a result war broke out. Ptolemy and Seleucus formed an allegiance and fought against Antiochus, but the price for Ptolemy's aid was the land of Israel. While the Jews were given autonomy over local concerns, they suffered greatly under the oppressive hand of the Ptolemaic Empire. They were forced annually to give an enormous amount of tribute and taxes to Egypt. The annual tribute was twenty talents of silver which was a huge fortune in ancient times. Non-payment would result in an Egyptian invasion of Israel and severe penalties upon its citizens. A tax collector named Joseph ben Toviyah volunteered to meet the king and made a deal with him to collect the taxes required by him from the Jews. King Ptolemy agreed to the arrangement and provided a battalion of 3,000 soldiers to assist him. Joseph then proceeded to greedily collect 7X more taxes from the people than was required previously. He gave the king the amount he had promised and kept the rest for himself.

In 199 BC Antiochus III the Great defeated the armies of Ptolemy V Philopator. He separated Israel from the Egyptian Empire. Overall he was kind to the Jews in Jerusalem and granted them special privileges.

Upon his death, he was succeeded by his son Seleucus IV. Seleucus IV was assassinated and succeeded by his younger brother Antiochus IV, surnamed Epiphanes. He attacked and conquered Egypt but was warned by Rome to either withdraw from Egypt or face an attack from Rome. He chose to withdraw. After this humiliating defeat, Antiochus IV turned north to Israel. He entered into Jerusalem through deception and flatteries. The people had no idea what was about to happen to them. They thought he was their friend but once inside, he attacked and massacred many of the people. He then defiantly entered the Temple sanctuary and looted it. He stole the golden altar, the golden lampstand, the menorah, the table of showbread, the golden cups, golden censers, golden crowns, ornaments, and the silver and gold vessels, and kept them for himself.

Then Antiochus IV issued a decree to all of the people of his realm, but focused primarily on the Jews, and ordered them to give up their religion and laws and become unified under the religion of the Greeks. On the fifteenth of Kislev [occurs on our Julian calendar between November 15th and December 7th] an abomination – i.e., an idol – was erected upon the altar, and beginning with the twenty-fifth of Kislev Antiochus IV had pigs sacrificed on the holy altar to the pagan deity, Zeus whom he identified with and felt he was a manifestation of. As a result of this desecration of their holy altar, a revolt began.

Beginning of the Jewish Revolt

Mattisyahu, an old priest, and his family lived in the small village of Modin near Jerusalem. One day the king's forces appeared and demanded that the townspeople offer a pig sacrifice on the altar. They tried to convince Mattisyahu to agree to their request and by so doing set an example for others in his community to follow. They were told if he and his sons would obey the king's order, they would be considered a friend of the king and would be rewarded greatly. Mattisyahu refused the offer. Then a Jew went to the altar to offer the sacrifice as requested by Antiochus IV in the sight of Mattisyahu. This act enraged Mattisyahu to the point that he picked up a sword and killed both the rebellious Jew and the king's messenger.

Antiochus' actions toward Judea and Jerusalem infuriated religious Jews, especially the family of Mattisyahu and his five sons: John, Simeon, Judas, Eleazar, and Jonathan. They tore their garments in a show of grief and put on sackcloth. They mourned for their temple and its beauty and glory that had been stolen. Mattisyahu then published a proclamation which read: "Whoever is zealous for the Torah and is steadfast in the Covenant let him follow me!"- Rabbi Goldwurm. He and his sons left everything they owned and fled to the mountains in the Judean desert and lived in the caves there where they could practice their religion in peace. About 6,000 people loyal to the Torah and the Covenant joined them there.

Men loyal to Antiochus IV Epiphanes found out what happened and told him that some of the Jews had fled to the mountains and were disobeying and resisting his orders. This was unacceptable so the king's forces. As a result, they began to seek out the Jews in the mountains. Mattisyahu knew he was locked in a struggle with the powers of darkness. The loyal Jews fought with him and began to destroy the pagan altars. Mattisyahu, knowing his death was imminent, told the loyal Jews to continue to resist the Syrian-Greek forces. With this, the die was cast; the revolt had begun.

Mattisyahu died shortly after the revolt began in 146 BC and his son Judas called Maccabee took over the fight as the leader. At first the Syrian-Greek army did not take this small band of Jews seriously. But Judas knew that strength came not from the number of men but from heaven. With determination and zeal for the Torah, the men with Judas killed 800 of the king's forces. Judas' victory over the Syrian-Greek army reached Antiochus IV and everyone around feared them. Antiochus gathered his entire army and prepared for combat against Judas and his forces. Despite being outnumbered, Judas held on to his faith in God and encouraged his men to pray. He set up a surprise attack against Antiochus' army. When the attack started, the Syrians started running away from the battle. The Jews destroyed the rear of the group and set fire to their camp. They then began to chase the fleeing army, killing 3,000 of the Syrian-Greek forces.

The Temple Rededication and the Mystery of the Oil

Judas and his men had fought many battles for three years. After their victory over the Syrian-Greek army in 164 BC, Judas and his men returned to Jerusalem and gathered at the Temple Mount. When they saw the condition of their abandoned temple, they began to grieve. Its sanctuary had a dilapidated appearance and the entire temple was overgrown with weeds. Its gates had been burned and its altar desecrated. The chambers that joined the temple were destroyed. Upon seeing this level of carnage, they tore their garments, covered their heads with ashes, and wept.

The destruction of the temple was predicted by Daniel the Prophet in Daniel 11:31-33. It says, "Forces from him will arise, desecrate the sanctuary fortress, and do away with the regular sacrifice. And they will set up the abomination of desolation. By smooth words he will turn to godlessness those who act wickedly toward the covenant, but the people who know their God will display strength and take action. Those who have insight among the people will give understanding to the many; yet they will fall by sword and by flame, by captivity and by plunder for many days".

Judah was determined to restore and rededicate the temple. He chose priests without blemish to cleanse and prepare the temple. The idols that Antiochus IV had placed in the temple were destroyed. The priests took the altar apart because it had been profaned and build a new one in time for the next service. They carried away the stones that had been defiled and took them to an unclean place in the northern wall of the temple court. They built up the holy places and sanctified the temple and its courts. They made new holy vessels. They fashioned a new temporary seven branch menorah out of seven wire spits since the golden one had been stolen. They brought in the altar of incense and put loaves of bread on the table of showbread. They put them in the temple in their prescribed place according to the Torah. They hung up the veil that separated the Holy of Holies from the holy place. With the work being completed, they began to search for the pure olive oil needed to light the menorah. The lighted menorah in the Temple represented the light of God's presence. It was also seen as a symbol of spiritual illumination through knowledge of the Torah. As the men searched for pure olive oil, every flask they found had its seal broken and its oil contaminated. Then miraculously they discovered one flask of oil that was strangely sealed with an unbroken seal of the Kohen Gadol [High Priest]. Sealing a flask of oil by the Kohen Gadol was not required nor was it a common practice. Thus it was with great joy the priests filled and lit the lamps on the menorah! Again a miracle took place. Instead of the oil lasting for only one day, it lasted for eight days. Copies of the Torah scroll were also made. The miracle of the oil was celebrated with an eight day Chanukah festival starting on the twenty-fifth of Kislev, 165 BC. The next day the daily burnt offering was offered up to God. The altar was rededicated and its rededication was celebrated for eight days with peace and thanksgiving offerings. Judah and the Sanhedrin decreed that Chanukah was to be celebrated yearly as "a message of hope". Its glow is to be a visual reminder to the people of the coming glow of their Messiah.

Mattisyahu, his five sons, and other Torah faithful Jews, were willing to risk their lives for the right to practice their religion and to resume temple services and sacrifices to God. Even in this day of encroaching darkness in the world, when Jewish people see the lights on their Hanukkiah during the eight days of Chanukah, they remember that it represents their redemption and freedom of worship. They praise God who helped them have victory over darkness.

A Story of a Divine Apparition

The book titled "Chanukah" was written in three parts, each by a different rabbi. The story recorded here was written by Rabbi Hersh Goldwurm in his section of the book.

The Ptolemies used the High Priest of Jerusalem to collect the taxes from the people. Chonyo III was an honest man who took over the position of tax collector which had been held by his great-grandfather and his father before him, but for some unknown reason he decided not to pay the annual tribute of twenty talents of silver that was required each year. As a result, Ptolemy threatened to invade Israel. In an attempt to calm him and avoid war, Chonyo's nephew got involved and gave the

Ptolemy expensive gifts. As a result of the success of his actions, he was given the job of tax collector. Unfortunately he aroused the enmity of a Temple official named Shimon when he disapproved of Shimon's bid to administer the markets of Jerusalem. Shimon became so angry that he went to see Apollonius, the Syrian governor of Phoenicia, with a concocted tale about a tremendous amount of wealth being kept in the temple treasury. When the king was told about the wealth of the temple treasury, he sent Heliodorus, his trusted official, to confiscate it. As soon as Heliodorus arrived in Jerusalem he met with the High Priest who told him the temple treasury did not contain the amount of money he had been led to believe. Heliodorus refused to believe him and attempted to enter the Temple. When he did, "a divine apparition in the form of a horse with an armed rider rushed at him and struck him with its forefeet. Then two young man appeared and flogged him mercilessly. He fell down unconscious and had to be carried away deathly sick. Upon recovering, Heliodorus hastened back to the king and attested to him about the Divine power that guarded the Temple in Jerusalem. Shimon and his party refused to be fazed by the miracle and asserted before the king that Chonyo has influenced Heliodorus to fabricate the entire incident. The rivalry between Chonyo's people and Shimon's men rose to such a pitch that the latter did not stop even at murder. At that point Chonyo felt it was his responsibility to bring the affair to a head and call the king's attention to Shimon's machinations". But before anything could be resolved, King Seleucus was assassinated and Antiochus IV Epiphanes took over in his place.

Yeshua Jesus Attends the Chanukah Feast

The Feast of Chanukah has several names. It has often been called the "Festival of Lights" but also the "Feast of Dedication". John 10:22-23 mentions the fact that Yeshua Jesus attended the Feast of Dedication in Jerusalem. It is a memorial to the Maccabeen revolt that occurred a hundred and sixty years before His birth! John 10:22-23 says, "At that time the Feast of the Dedication took place at Jerusalem; it was winter, and Jesus was walking in the temple in the portico of Solomon. The portico of Solomon was located on the eastern part of the walkway surrounding the outer court of Herod's temple. Yeshua used this area as a place for informal teaching. It was at here that the Jews [priests] asked Yeshua if He was the Messiah. In verse 24 of John the Jews queries about Yeshua are written: 1) "How long will You keep us in suspense? and 2) If You are the Christ, tell us plainly". When He responded, "I and the Father are one", the Jews picked up stones again to stone Him – John 10:31. It may be that they thought when the Messiah came, He would help them defeat the Romans and restore their freedoms in much the same way that Judas Maccabee did. They either did not know or understand the prophecy by Daniel which specifically points to the date when the Jewish Messiah would arrive and the fact that the Messiah would be cut off – Daniel 9:26. They did not realize that Chanukah would come a second time, two hundred years later, in 70 AD and destroy their temple again. Yeshua Jesus told His disciples that an anti-Christ would come and repeat the actions of Antiochus IV [during the period of time called "the time of Jacob's Trouble" and the Tribulation Period]; and that He will slay him with the "breath of His mouth".

Yeshua did not come at His first coming to defend the Jews against the Romans. He came to defeat the enemies who could steal a man's soul. It will be when He comes with His saints at His second coming that He will defeat the enemies of God – Revelation 17:14. "And the beast was seized, and with him the false prophet who performed the signs in his presence, by which he deceived those who had received the mark of the beast and those who worshiped his image; those two were thrown alive into the lake of fire which burns with brimstone. And the rest were killed with the sword which came from the mouth of Him who sat on the horse, and all the birds were filled with their flesh" – Revelation 19:20-21. [Yeshua] Jesus is the light of the world – John 1:6-9, 9:5 who came to bear witness to the light.

When it all looked hopeless, God raised up a people who were loyal to Him and His law to fight for their freedom to worship Him. In the story of Chanukah He rose up an old priest named Mattisyahu and his five sons. Mattisyahu told the people that what was happening was not acceptable. He would not surrender to Antiochus IV Epiphanes' orders and pagan values. He believed God had called him to defend God's holy name and the truth of His Word. As Christians, we must do no less. We must let our "light shine before men in such a way that they may see your good works and glorify your Father who is in heaven" – Matthew 5:16. As we read Matthew 24 concerning the end-times, we can almost hear Yeshua Jesus warning His disciples that Chanukah would happen again and the temple would once more be destroyed. This happened just as He predicted in 70 AD. Some teachers believe it will happen a third time during the Tribulation Period when the anti-Christ will come and repeat the actions of Antiochus IV Epiphanes in the time of the third temple. I Thessalonians 5:2-5 tells us that we are not in darkness and that the day will not overtake us like a thief in the night. We are all sons of light and sons of the day. We, the redeemed, can comfort each other with these words.

How Chanukah is Celebrated Today

Chanukah is a time to celebrate thankfulness, give praise to God, and be joyful. A nine branched menorah is used called a hanukkiah. The center candle is called a Shamash or servant candle. It is the first candle to be lit. It is used to light up all eight of the other candles, one for each day for eight days. The candles which represent light and hope are lit from left to right as each of the eight days of the festival unfold. This type of menorah is only used in the celebration of Chanukah otherwise a seven-branched menorah is used. Each branch of the seven-branched menorah is said to represent the seven feasts described in the book of Leviticus. Many Christians, however, believe the seven-branched menorah represents the seven churches in the book of Revelation.

Fun with Family and Friends

1. Place a hanukkiah near a window so once lit the candle light can be seen outside.
2. Tell the story of the miracle of Chanukah.
3. Share the importance of standing up for your faith and beliefs in the face of hardship and pressure from others, like the Maccabees did.
4. Pray and thank God for the meal and His daily provisions.
5. Eat foods cooked in oil such as, Latkes [potato pancakes] and jelly-filled donuts.

Two Fun Games to Play:

1. Children and adults enjoy playing The Dreidel Game. A dreidel is a four-sided top with a different Hebrew letter on each side. The letters are: nun, gimmel, hey and shin. The letters spell out the sentence: "A great miracle happened here"; referring to the Maccabee's victory over the greatest army in the world; that of Antiochus IV Epiphanes. Gold wrapped chocolate candies or pennies are used as "money" in this game. At the end of the game, each child receives a gift.
2. The White Elephant Game. As adults, we enjoy playing a white elephant game. Each person wraps up a white elephant gift and puts it in a pile with the other gifts.. The funnier the better. If purchased, it can not cost more than $10.00. Numbers are written on a small, folded piece of paper, one for each player, and put in a bowl. Each player takes a number from the bowl. The one who has number one goes first. He/she selects one of the wrapped gifts, but does NOT unwrap it. Person number two can either take that gift from person number one or select a different gift from the pile. If person number two takes the gift from person number one, he/she can select another one from the pile but not open it. Whoever gets a gift that has gone around the group three times gets to open the gift and keep it.

ANCIENT JEWISH BRIDE

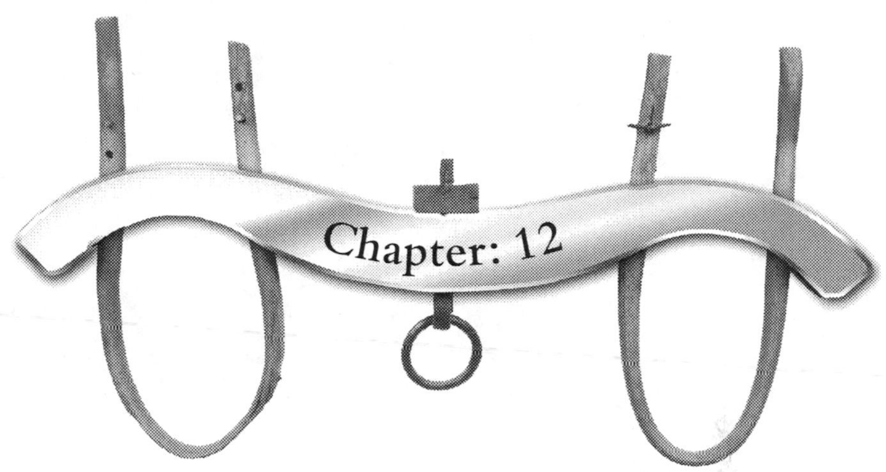

The Ancient Jewish Wedding and the Feast of the Lord

A wedding ceremony is an event that is looked forward to with much anticipation and joy. In Western culture this ceremony is performed when an individual falls in love with the person they believe to be their soul-mate. Too often, however, they do not wait for the Lord to choose their life mate for them. They fail to recognize the difference between love and need. They often do not know that marriage is meant to be an intimate covenant relationship between the bride, the groom and God. This type of relationship must be taken very seriously before two people enter into it. A covenant is not the same as a contract. A contract is a temporary agreement between two people, both of whom do not fully know or trust the other to do what has been committed to. A covenant by comparison is a permanent agreement that is based on love and trust between two parties. It does not expire. A covenant marriage is meant to be a reflection of the relationship between God and Israel and the Lord Yeshua and His church.

On the sixth day of Creation, God kneeled down and created man with His two hands. He created man in His own image and put in him a living soul. When the Lord God created man, He said, "It is not good for man to be alone; I will make him a helper suitable to him"... So the

Lord God caused a deep sleep to fall upon the man, and he slept; then He took one of his ribs and closed up the flesh at that place. The Lord God fashioned into a woman the rib which He had taken from the man, and brought her to the man" – Genesis 2:18, 21.

The first wedding is believed to have taken place on the sixth day in the Garden of Eden after God brought the woman He had made from Adam's rib to Adam. Adam was so excited when he saw the woman God had created for him that the first words out of his mouth were "bone of my bones, and flesh of my flesh!" Genesis 2:24 reveals God's will for His children when He said, ..."a man shall leave his father and his mother, and be joined to his wife, and they shall become one flesh". So after the marriage was performed by God they were told to "be fruitful and multiply and fill the earth" with their offspring– Genesis 1:28. The Jewish sages believe these actions by God made Satan very jealous. He resented the mystical union God had made between the man and the woman He created; a union in which they were the only living beings able to produce another living being with an eternal soul.

The Jewish Commentary on the Torah suggests that God created Adam and Eve as one person with two faces. There are two thoughts as to what this means. One is that a man and his future wife are in heaven but are divided in half. When they come to earth they must find and join with their soul mate. When they marry their other half they truly become one whole person. The second thought is this is a figure of speech, a metaphor. It is comparing the intimate emotional bond between two people as being so close they become like one person. That is what God desires for a married couple. His desire is that they become so close to each other in love, respect, faith, needs, and trust that they reflect each other. This allows each person to meet the needs of the other in the marriage relationship. The woman was made to walk by her husband's side as an equal partner in marriage, not one to be treated as his slave or as his property. This beautiful sentiment is manifested in the Jewish wedding. A holy marriage is meant to be a pattern and reflection of God's love for the people He created. Thus the ancient Jewish wedding was meant to be the model of love and joy Yeshua Jesus has for His bride, both now and at the end of the age.

In the ancient Hebrew culture when a son reached the age of majority for marriage he would speak to his father about his desire to marry and start his own family. When he approached his father, his father would show his approval by laying his hand on his son's head and blessing him; a tradition that goes back as far as the time of Abraham. After the father gave his son his blessing, the process of wife selection would begin. It was customary in that culture, as well as among many devout Orthodox Jewish families today, that either the father of the bridegroom or a matchmaker he had employed would select a bride for his son, just as Abraham sent his servant to find a wife for his son Isaac. Usually the young men and women grew up living separately and therefore did not know each other. The bridal candidates had to be from an honorable Jewish family and of good character and inner beauty. Once the bride was chosen, the bridegroom would go to visit his perspective bride and bring with him a written marriage contract called a *Ketubah*. It contained the promises made by the groom to the bride and her family. The groom stipulated the contents of the bride's dowry and pledged to support his wife. When he arrived at her house, she had the choice to either open the door to let him in or to keep the door closed as a sign of her rejection of him as a spouse. If she let him in, he came in and pledged his love for her. He then asked her to become his bride [*Kallah*]. If she chose to accept his offer of marriage, the Ketubah was presented to the bride-to-be and her father to be kept and cherished. It was meant to protect the status of the bride as they entered into marriage. Many Christians believe God gave us the Bible as our Ketubah.

A type of screening test to confirm the worthiness of a potential groom was sometimes employed by the father of the bride-to-be as follows. He would set a variety of foods in front of the potential groom. The prospective father-in-law would watch to see if the young man knew the correct blessings to give and in what order to give them. If he failed the test, he was not allowed to proceed with the betrothal. If he passed the test, the commitment of marriage was sealed by the bridegroom's offering of a glass of wine to the bride and her father. This cup was called "the Cup of Acceptance". When the bride and her father drink the wine, it signaled their acceptance and was considered to be a covenant based in blood. After that, the couple were said to be betrothed/married even though the marriage had not been consummated. The couple were then considered to be set apart as holy and sacred for each other. After the pledge, the bride-to-be and the bridegroom were not free to seek out another partner. The bridegroom gave his betrothed the gift of a golden betrothal ring as his pledge of love and were legally recognized as married. The couple then separated for a period of time in order for him to prepare a lovely new home for his bride. During this period of separation the bride would prepare herself for the wedding. Imagine how Miriam [Mary] must have felt when the angel approached her about becoming the mother of the Messiah! One can be certain that both she and Joseph had heard the story for years in the synagogue about the virgin birth of the Messiah. Still, when she was approached by the angel what strength of faith she demonstrated when her answer was yes! She knew the consequences that would happen to her if she was determined to be pregnant outside her betrothal to Joseph. It was little wonder when Joseph found out she was pregnant that he wanted to divorce her quietly [only the man could ask for a divorce]. His first thought must have been that she had broken the blood vow of marriage to him. The emotional hurt he felt must have been unbearable until the angel came and told him not to be afraid to take Miriam [Mary] as his wife "for the child who has been conceived in her is of the Holy Spirit"- Matthew 1:20. What strength of love, character, and restraint he showed! It is no wonder that God chose this couple to be the human instruments through whom His Son, the Messiah, would to born on the earth.

Under normal conditions a bride would spend her time letting go of the things of her past and make herself beautiful and ready for her bridegroom. During this time the bridegroom would send gifts of love to his bride to encourage her and reassure her of his love for her. The bridegroom would understandably be excited but neither he nor his bride knew the day or the hour of the bridegroom's return for the wedding; only the groom's father knew. The bride goes about her daily tasks but with a longing heart toward the day her bridegroom would return. When the time for the wedding was close, the bridegroom would carry a sprig of myrtle in his hands and ask his friends to be groomsmen at his wedding. When the day finally arrived, the groom dressed in his royal clothes [a white robe called a *kittel*] and placed a garland of myrtle and roses on his head in the form of a crown like a king. He and his groomsmen then proceeded in a procession to the home of his bride, usually at dusk, with lit torches, singing songs of praise to God, and blowing shofars. The joyful sounds and sights could be seen and heard across the hillsides. The bridesmaid on watch alerts the bridal party by crying out "behold the groom"! He is coming to take his bride to her wedding and new home. The bride was dressed in her most beautiful raiment and was adorned like a queen. Her golden crown depicted the walls of Jerusalem. When her bridesmaids saw the groom approaching, they would bring the bride to her bridegroom. The bride wore a veil over her face which represented her modesty and purity. When the bride and groom looked at each other, the bridegroom asked his bride to remove the veil from over her face. While this may seem like a strange request, the history of this request may go back to the time of Jacob when he was tricked by his Uncle Laban into marrying Leah when he thought he was marrying Rachel. In truth, had Jacob not tricked Esau out of his birthright, Esau as the first born would have married Leah who was the firstborn child of Laban, and Jacob could have legitimately married Rachel as the second born.

Today, the bride and groom are raised up on chairs that are covered with a temporary canopy called a *Chuppah* which is made from a prayer shawl. In the past, an elaborate chuppah was the focal point. In either case, this covering represented the bridal chamber. The couple was carried through the village where they were seen as a king and queen. Torches lit their path. Their music and songs could be heard throughout the countryside as they journeyed to the home the bridegroom has prepared for her.

At the wedding the bride and groom walked together as king and queen though today they can't be crowned since there is no longer a temple. She carried a bouquet of myrtle which was a symbol of love. As was customary, a blessing was recited over the myrtle and a dance was performed with myrtle branches before the bride. This was thought to bring her happiness. A canopy [*chuppah*], overhung with myrtle, was erected for the bride. The wedding flowers were meant to remind the couple of the beauty of the Garden of Eden and the joyful moments at Mount Sinai when God gave the Jewish people the Torah and married them.

Pastor Biltz offered an interesting insight into the meaning of Hebrew numbers. The Hebrew number for blood is forty-four. The number for a father is forty + 1 and the number for a mother is two + one. When they are added together you get 44. Since life is in the blood, a baby can only be conceived by the union of a man's sperm and a woman's ovum. The Jewish sages believe if a married couple do not have God in the center of their relationship, the couple will consume each other like an unrestrained fire. If

God is in the middle of their relationship, meaning the husband and his wife are equally yoked then their relationship will be one of closeness and love.

The wedding ceremony unites the groom and the bride and sets them apart from all others, just as the Sabbath day is separated from the rest of the week. The groom enters the chuppah first and walks out in front to meet his bride and together they enter the chuppah which represents the bridal chamber and is a symbol of their joining as one. The couple's life together is then blessed by the rabbi. In modern times, the entire wedding is performed under the chuppah. It is believed that it is during this time that the couple is particularly close to God, and the gates of heaven are open so one's prayers are easily accepted. The bride walks around her husband seven times. As the bride encircles her husband with her love and envelopes him with affection the walls that protect his heart begin to crumble. He lets his defenses and vulnerabilities down and begins to feel like he is the center of her world. Psalm 45 and Isaiah 61:10 – 62:5 are read and the ceremony concludes with a sevenfold blessing that is usually sung by a close relative or cantor. The number seven alludes to the numerical value of the Hebrew word echad which means "one".

The bride now goes toward her new life with her groom, and as she does, everything old and familiar to her is left behind. The groom now declares all he owns is also hers, his bride. Then they lift up a glass of wine to seal their marriage covenant and break the glass afterwards. Breaking the glass at this moment of happiness and celebration is a reminder to the bride and groom that not everything in the course of a marriage is joyful; that one must always trust God regardless of the circumstances they find themselves in. They need to realize that even in a good marriage there are various times when problems will arise that challenge the relationship. At these times some couples become so overwhelmed and disappointed with their partner that they decide to break up the marriage. To avoid this type of heartbreak and pain, the couple must remember the marriage covenant they made between themselves and God, and work together toward finding solutions for the problems they confront rather than running away from them. God can turn even the negative things of their life into blessings and opportunities for growth.

During the festivities they quietly slip away for a time of seclusion to the bridegroom's chamber. They lock the doors from the inside, set a guard by the door on the outside to ensure their privacy, and consummate their marriage relationship. As the two are now one, they reflect on the significance of the day. Afterwards, on a signal from the groom, the guard opens the door and the bride and bridegroom participate in the marriage supper with their families, attendants of the bride and groom, and their invited guests. Everyone celebrates the happiness of the new couple as they start their married life together. At this point the celebrants dance around the couple as an expression of support and a second blessing is given for the couple.

The Wedding at Cana

The great wedding celebration took place for seven days! As we think about this, we reflect on the miracle at the marriage in Cana. The Scripture says it was on the third day of the wedding celebration that the wine ran out. Since the whole village was usually present at the wedding this could be very embarrassing to the bridegroom's family and the bridal couple. It says that Jesus was at the wedding on this day with His disciples when He was approached by His mother, Mary, who told Him the wine had run out. This was when Jesus told the servants to "fill the waterpots with water" and the water became wine. Why was this important enough to be mentioned? Could there be more than the lack of wine to this story? Yes, Jesus performed a miracle, but what else made this significant? Notice what the headwaiter said to the bridegroom. He said, "Every man serves the good wine first, and when the people have drunk freely, then he serves the poorer wine; but you have kept the good wine until now". It has been written that wine glasses were purple in color like an amethyst. It was therefore a common practice during an important event like a wedding that the wine would be watered down, especially after everyone had been drinking for three days. But the wine Jesus miraculous made was better than the good wine that was served during the first day. We as believers know that our faith is like new wine [new life] in new wineskins. We don't go back to the old way of believing and waiting once we have met Yeshua Jesus as our Lord and Savior.

After the week long celebration, the bride and her bridegroom begin their married life in the home the bridegroom had prepared for them during their long separation. Each took up the role God had given them, a role in which they loved each other and honored their union before God. When God blesses them with children, they were to teach them the faith of their fathers and of the Torah. As they and their children deepen their faith through the study God's Word, they all grow in love and in the awe of God.

Summary of the Stages of the Jewish Wedding

1. **The Proposal** – The bridegroom [the Chatan] prepares a Ketubah [marriage contract] which is given to the bride-to-be [the Kallah] and her father once the prospective bride says "yes" to the bridegroom's proposal. It contains promises made by the groom and a dowry, to compensate the bride and her parents should the bridegroom renege on his promise of marriage or dies before it can be consummated.
2. **Acceptance and Betrothal** – A cup of wine called the Cup of Acceptance is poured by the groom-to-be for the bride-to-be to drink. If she drinks it, she has accepted the bridegroom's proposal of marriage. At this point, even though the marriage has not been consummated, the couple are considered married. The bride is now set apart from other potential mates and is sealed for her husband only. Neither the bride nor the groom is any longer free to seek out other partners once the betrothal period of at least one year has begun.
3. **The Groom Prepares a Home for His Bride** – The bridegroom leaves his betrothed to prepare a home for her. He promises to return and receive her unto himself. The place he prepares is attached to the groom's father's house, so only the father can say when it has been completed. The bridegroom leaves a special gift [a matan] for his bride to let her know he loves her. She prepares herself for her new life with her husband and for leaving behind her father's house and all she had known up to this point.
4. **The Wedding** - The groom returns with his friends, singing and blowing the shofar. He has come for his bride! He and his bride go to the wedding chamber to consummate their marriage. A friend of the groom serves as a guard at the door so the couple will not be disturbed as the marriage is consummated. When the groom gives the signal, his friend opens the door and the groom leads his wife under the canopy. There they celebrate their union and share the marriage

supper with their family and friends. For seven days the wedding celebration includes eating, dancing, and drinking wine. Afterwards the groom takes his bride to the home he has prepared for her. When they arrive home she is greeted and accepted as part of his family.

Reviving Biblical Wedding Customs in Preparation for the Third Temple

Reuven Prager, a tailor in Israel, has done exhaustive research on the ancient Jewish wedding customs and "has a passion for restoring them". Through his research he discovered four forgotten wedding items and has learned how to recreate the four items that were used in ancient weddings! One item was the bridal crown. He was able to duplicate it, with the aid of a skilled goldsmith, in polished brass. He said "the kallah [bride] wore a crown of gold depicting the walls of Jerusalem" until the temple was destroyed in 70AD. Until the third temple is built, a bride can not wear a crown made of gold but can wear one made from a metal of lesser value such as brass. The crown of the groom was made of roses and myrtle. The myrtle is a beautiful flowering plant with five petals which represent grace and love. The groom can not be crowned as a king until after the third temple is built.

Contemporary weddings focus on the chuppah/canopy that is usually made from a tallit [prayer shawl] "that is suspended on four poles". In the time of the second temple the chuppah chatanim was "shaped like a dome". It was made of "crimson silk decorated with fine beaten goldwork". Mr. Prager made the dome and its four ornately carved wood poles that suspend the chuppah chatanim.

The last item took Mr. Prager nine-and-a-half years and a cost of $30,000.00 to make. It was the Aperion. An Aperion was used to carry the bride to the chuppah chatanim. Prager had to send a man to Damascus via Amman, Jordan to obtain a roll of silk and gold brocade material for sale on the black market. It had been made for King Fahd of Saudi Arabia and cost Mr. Prager a small fortune to obtain! He used it to cover the center section of the front doors and the center sides of the Aperion. With the aid of upholsterers, the interior of the Aperion was fashioned from purple velvet, just as described in the Song of Songs.

The bride sat inside the Aperion like a Queen. Groomsmen, dressed in deep blue clothing of the period, carried the Aperion by attached poles, similar in style to those attached to the Ark of the Covenant. Additional groomsmen blew shofars in front of the Aperion as the joyful procession made its way to the chuppah and the wedding ceremony.

Note: Pictures of the bride's crown, aperion and chuppah chatanim taken by Mr. Prager are in Appendix 1 at the back of this book.

The Significance of the Flowering White Myrtle Plant

The common white myrtle flower has five petals, five sepals and numerous yellow-tipped stamen. It is found in the Mediterranean region of the Middle East. This star-shaped white myrtle flower is often used in the bride's bridal bouquet. The groom wears a garland of myrtle on his head. In Jewish mysticism, the myrtle represents the phallic as a masculine force. The groom is therefore often given sprigs of myrtle after the marriage ceremony as he enters the bridal chamber with his bride.

This flower is often given as a wedding gift to a newly married couple because the white myrtle flower is believed to be associated with marital fidelity, love, good luck, prosperity, and a long, happy life.

In the Scriptures the number five represents God's goodness and grace. Thus, mankind is the recipient of God's grace, so the wedding is a visual picture of God's grace toward the marriage of man and a woman.

The myrtle is one of the four species used to make the lulav that is waved during the Feast of Tabernacles. As one may recall, the lulav is waved in all four directions of the compass– N, S, E, and W and up and down to show that one can not escape God for He is everywhere. Additionally, it is also believed to represent the good deeds performed by an individual despite the fact that he or she does not have knowledge gained from studying the Torah.

Note: Sadly, in the Autumn of 2017, the Sanhedrin announced that Jews who become Christians in Israel will not have their marriages recognized. These leaders are repeating a pattern of rejection from the first century when neither the Messianic assemblies nor Yeshua Jesus was accepted by the majority of Jews in spiritual leadership.

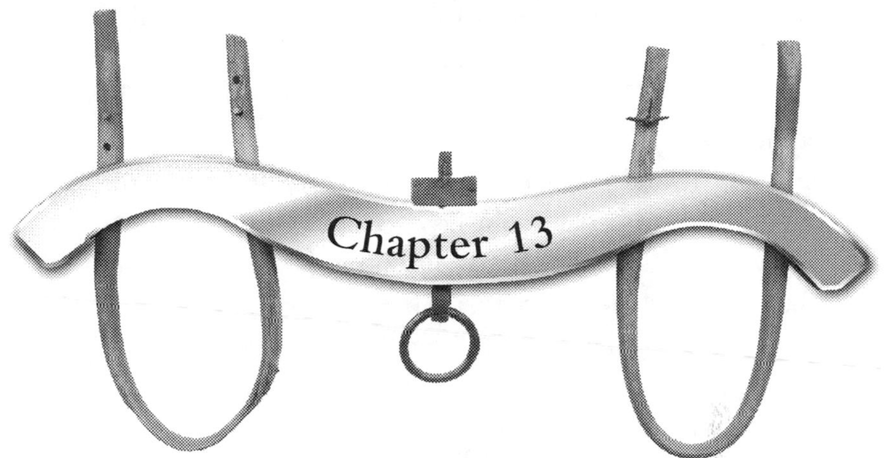

The Marriage Supper of the Lamb

There is disagreement among Christians leaders as to exactly what the Marriage Supper of the Lamb is and when it will occur. Jesus compared the wedding feast given by a king to the kingdom of heaven in Matthew 22:2-14 and Luke 14:16-24. The king invited many quests to the wedding but they gave reasons to excuse themselves. The king sent his slaves to gather people from the streets of the city to attend the wedding. When they arrived, he gave each of his guests white garments to wear. When one person tried to enter into the wedding feast without the proper garment, the king asked him why he had came without a wedding garment. It says the man was surprised. The object of this parable was to show that the man was trying to attend the wedding feast based in his own righteousness. This is like trying to get into heaven through one's own good works and righteousness, rather than through the blood, righteousness, and acceptance of Messiah Jesus.

Some born-again believers connect being taken up into heaven in the Rapture to the timing of the Marriage Supper of the Lamb. Other believers deny having belief in the Rapture because they say it is not specifically spelled out in Scripture. Yet both I Thessalonians and I Corinthians describe what is commonly termed as the Rapture of the church, but neither of the verses says anything about the Marriage Supper of the Lamb being held just after the Rapture. Some of the confusion about the Rapture may be linked to the English language since the word Rapture comes from Latin.

I Thessalonians 4:16-18 says, "For the Lord Himself will descend from heaven with a shout, with the voice of the archangel and with the trumpet of God, and the dead in Christ will rise first. Then we who are alive and remain will be caught up together with them in the clouds to meet the Lord in the air, and so we shall always be with the Lord. Therefore comfort one another with these words".

I Corinthians 15:51-53 says, "Behold, I tell you a mystery; we will not all sleep, but we will all be changed, in a moment, in the twinkling of an eye, at the last trumpet; for the trumpet will sound, and the dead will be raised imperishable, and we will be changed. For this perishable must put on the imperishable, and this mortal must put on immortality".

There is a disagreement between the timing of the Rapture and the timing of the Marriage Supper of the Lamb. Some believe that the redeemed of the Lord will not experience any of the Tribulation Period because they believe it is exclusively a "Time of Jacob's Trouble", referring to non-redeemed Israel. Some believe that even the redeemed will experience the first three and a half years of the seven-year Tribulation Period. Still others say the Rapture won't occur until the end of the Tribulation Period. Since the Marriage Supper of the Lamb is not mentioned, it again appears that the timing of the Marriage Supper of the Lamb is independent of the timing of the Rapture.

Most Christians have been taught that Yeshua Jesus will receive His bride in the Rapture which will occur at some point [either pre, middle, or post Tribulation] during the 7-year Tribulation Period on earth. The redeemed will stand before the Judgment Seat of Christ to give an account of the deeds they have done while in the body -II Corinthians 5:10, be rewarded with various crowns for their service to the Lord while on earth, and afterwards enjoy the Marriage Supper of the Lamb. This teaching separates the timing of the Rapture from the Marriage Supper of the Lamb. The questions I asked myself are: 1) What is the Marriage Supper of the Lamb? 2) When does the Marriage Supper occur? 3) If there is no marriage in heaven, why would there be a marriage supper? 4) Why do the Scriptures speak of the wife of the Lamb and not the Bride of Christ [the Lamb]?

According to some researchers and scholars the teaching of the church concerning the Marriage Supper of the Lamb is incorrect. They believe that Yeshua never intended for the redeemed that have been taken up in the Rapture to be sitting back and enjoying themselves at the Marriage Supper in heaven while people still on the earth are suffering during the reign of the anti-Christ and the seven years of the Tribulation Period. They believe the redeemed will join with Yeshua in their glorified bodies to destroy the enemies of Israel in the great battle for Jerusalem - Zechariah 14:5 and avenge the blood of martyred saints – Revelation 6:10. In Psalm 50:5, the Lord says, "Gather My godly ones to Me, Those who have made a covenant with Me by sacrifice." This theme is similar to the one found in Matthew 24:31 which says, "And He [Yeshua Jesus] will send forth His angels with a great trumpet and they will gather together His elect from the four winds, from one end of the sky to the other". It is believed that these verses are speaking of the Battle of Armageddon; that this last great battle will put an end to Satan's rule on earth through the anti-Christ. Joel 2:11 speaks of the Day of the Lord and an impending battle against the enemies of God's people. Is it possible that the Rapture of the church and the Marriage Supper of the Lamb are both referring to war? Revelation 19:9 says, "Then he [an angel] said to me, Write, 'Blessed are those who are invited to the marriage supper of the Lamb.'" Verses 14-15 says, And the armies which are in heaven ["the mighty ones" referred to in Isaiah 13:3], clothed in fine linen [which represents the righteous deeds of God's people], white and clean, were following Him on white horses. From His mouth comes a sharp sword, so that with it He may strike down the nations, and He will rule them with a rod of iron; and He treads the wine press of the fierce wrath of God, the Almighty" ... And I saw the beast and the kings of the earth and their armies gathered to make war against Him who was sitting on the horse and against His army – Revelation 19:19. They believe the bride [the redeemed church of Yeshua] and her bridegroom [Yeshua] prepare for war just after the Rapture. Therefore the Marriage Supper of the Lamb is about the redeemed in their glorified bodies getting prepared for the battle for Jerusalem. This incorruptible army will return to earth with Messiah to fight with Him against the enemies of God on the "Day of the Lord".

Perry Stone of Manna Fest Ministries appears to have a different take on the Marriage Supper of the Lamb. He believes it will occur in heaven during the seventh year that the Tribulation is happening on earth. He agrees that the bride is the church and the bridegroom is Yeshua. He bases the period of time of the Marriage Supper on the ancient Jewish wedding. When a groom marries the bride he had chosen, he was given a year free from military service or any other work, according to the Law of Moses. During the first year of their marriage the couple would get to know each other, consummate their marriage contract [called a "Blood Covenant" in Hebrew], and have time to start a family. It was considered a sabbatical year of rest. Stone does not mention the Marriage Supper being connected to war or the Rapture.

Another view of the Marriage Supper suggests that the Rapture will remove believers in Yeshua Jesus and take them to heaven while the seven year Tribulation period is happening on earth. Afterward, Yeshua will bring the redeemed back to earth with Him at His Second Coming where they will be introduced to those who survived the Tribulation Period. It will be then that the glorious celebration of the Marriage Supper of the Lamb will take place.

But what is the Marriage Supper of the Lamb? If we follow the historical pattern, it will be a Seder meal like the one established in the books of Exodus and Leviticus. Tom Stapleton believes the Last Supper instituted by Yeshua as one of His last acts while on the earth was a type of Marriage Supper and that the Marriage Supper of the Lamb will be a Seder meal on the new earth. He believes this will occur during the Feast of Unleavened Bread.

A Glorious View of the Wedding Supper of the Lord

Susan Davis, a modern day prophet, describes the Marriage Supper of the Lamb in heaven as dictated to her "from the heart of God". She describes the wedding supper as a glorious experience that Yeshua and His Father have prepared for the bride. She describes the wedding supper as follows: "The table is lavishly prepared: every accoutrement will be provided...MY children will be seated in front of a place setting with their name lettered in pure gold. Each place setting will have golden utensils embedded with jewels. There will be solid gold plates also studded with jewels. The tablecloth will be of pure silk spun with golden threads. Light will shine through the weave. The cups will be gold with jewels around the rim. Each place setting will have a gift especially for each child; ... a precious reminder of MY relationship with this child... Each child will have an angel who waits on him. MY table will be full of light: candles of light, beautiful Menorahs...the bride will see ME in all My Glory...MY beauty will shine through and MY Love will flow out and overwhelm all attending. I will present MY bride with a ring. Our names will be written on this ring. Flowers and music will be everywhere. Everyone will sing praises to the King...MY children will also be shown their mansions... nothing can compare to the magnificence of what MY bride has in store for her. These mansions are living. They take My children to and from wonderful places for MY children to enjoy and experience. We will share these adventures together. MY Love will surround their every move. Laughter, love, and joy are the rewards of these eternal homes, joy unspeakable, everlasting delight". I Corinthians 2:9 gives us a hint that confirms this view. It says, "But as it is written, eye has not seen, nor ear heard, neither have entered into the heart of man, the things which God has prepared for them that love Him".

A Solution to the Marriage Supper of the Lamb Question

Is it possible that the Marriage Supper of the Lamb is different from many of the thoughts that have been proposed at this point? Let's look once more at the ancient Jewish wedding and how it is reflective of the future for believers in Messiah. First, Messiah asks one question, do you accept Me as your Lord and Savior? If the answer is a heart-felt yes, then He considers Himself betrothed to you as His bride, you and those who have accepted Him as Messiah, Savior, and Lord. In the ancient Jewish wedding the bride begins to prepare herself for her wedding after having accepted the proposal by her bridegroom-to-be which is marked by sharing a cup of wine. The acceptance of the wine represents the beginning of the betrothal period and seals the covenant made between the bride and the groom. Afterwards the bridegroom leaves for awhile to prepare a home for His bride. To assure her of his love, the groom gives her a golden ring and gifts in his absence. At some point, perhaps a year or more, the bridegroom returns for his bride. This is what Yeshua Jesus did when He gave the gift of the Holy Spirit and the Scriptures to His bride to comfort her in His absence and as He reassured her with these words: "Do not let your heart be troubled; believe in God, believe also in Me. In My Father's house are many dwelling places [mansions]; if it were not so, I would have told you; for I go to prepare a place for you. If I go and prepare a place for you, I will come again and receive you to Myself, that where I am, there you may be also" – John 14:1-3. Being assured of His love, the redeemed begin to prepare for their wedding as they look for His return.

At some point in time which only the Father knows, Yeshua, our bridegroom, will return. Meanwhile, before the final gathering of believers, both Jew and Gentile, who washed their clothing clean in the blood of the Lamb during the Tribulation Period, those who had accepted Him before the Tribulation, will be called to join Him in the Rapture and be given the gift of a glorified body in a moment, in a twinkling of an eye. The new heavenly bodies given to the redeemed will be incorruptible and can never be destroyed. We will then join Yeshua Jesus in the battle against the enemies of Israel and of God. Yeshua Jesus will win!! We will rule and reign with Him on the new earth for a thousand years from the city of Jerusalem, and then Satan will be released for a season of time. This will occur to prove once and for all that even when mankind is given a perfect environment in which to live, and the holy Savior to follow, some people will chose to sin. They will not accept Yeshua Jesus as their Lord and Savior, just like they rejected God in the Garden of Eden. Thus the earth will need to be cleansed. Satan and all other non-believers are separated from God throughout eternity as their actions have demanded and the earth will be made new. Now the bride is ready for the wedding. Revelation 19:7 says "... the marriage of the Lamb has come and His bride has made herself ready". Then verse 9 says "... 'Blessed are those who are invited to the marriage supper of the Lamb'".

With having a clearer understanding of the ancient Jewish wedding and the fact it is a dress rehearsal for the heavenly wedding, what are the answers to the questions asked most often concerning the Marriage

Supper of the Lamb? The following thoughts are an attempt to answer the questions that are most often asked. 1) Is the Marriage Supper of the Lamb Communion? No, but Communion is a type of Marriage Supper for those who have accepted Yeshua as their Lord and Savior. 2) Revelation speaks of the wife of the Lamb but not a bride, so has the church simply used the term bride as a representation of something else? Yeshua refers to the bride as the redeemed, and as His wife, after the Millennial Reign. 3) If there is no wedding in heaven, how can there be a Marriage Supper? The marriage supper will occur on the new earth, not in heaven, after Satan, the beast, the false prophet, and their followers have been cast into the lake of fire – Revelation 20:10. 4) The Marriage Supper will be like the Seder meal that takes on the Feast of Tabernacles after the earth has been cleansed at the end of the Millennial reign. It may be held during the Feast of Sukkot. The rationale for the Marriage Supper being held during Sukkot is that this feast is hidden in the number seven. Sukkot is the seventh feast and a celebration of the crowning of Yeshua Jesus as the King of kings. The number seven would connect it with the seventh day which is the Sabbath and the end of the week of Creation. Sukkot is also the seventh month on the Hebrew calendar. Putting the sevens together, we get 777. The Sabbath is the first feast God blessed and its title contains His holy name. Sukkot is the last of the pilgrimage feasts when everyone is required to go to Jerusalem. Revelation 15:4 confirms that all nations will come and worship before the Lamb of God for all He has done.

The following sequence of events may give further illumination on these questions as to the timing: 1) Messiah marries believers through their acceptance of Him as their personal Savior and Lord, 2) the Rapture of redeemed believers takes place in a moment, in a twinkling of an eye, 3) The Tribulation Period brings the remainder of the Bride to Yeshua, 4) Redeemed return to earth at the end of the Tribulation with Yeshua at His Second Coming and participate with Him in the war of Gog and Magog against the enemies of God and Israel. 5) Fire will come down from heaven and all the enemies of God will be destroyed, 6) The Millennial Reign of Messiah on earth will commence, 7) Satan will be released for a season, 8) Satan and his cohorts are thrown into the Lake of Fire, along with his followers. 9) The bride of Yeshua will enjoy the

Marriage Supper of the Lamb with their bridegroom, and 10) Sabbath rest in heaven for eternity.

The joyful Marriage Supper of the Lamb will most likely occur when Yeshua Jesus and His saints are able to enjoy the new earth which has been cleansed from all sin. Being totally free of sin cannot happen until after Satan, his cohorts, and his evil followers have been destroyed and when all of the redeemed by Yeshua's blood will be gathered together to enjoy this feast. This explains the timing of the Marriage Supper of the Lamb. This also answers the question about there being no marriage in heaven. The Marriage Supper is held on the new earth and not in heaven as some have proposed.

As we try to define exactly what the Marriage Supper of the Lamb is and when it will occur, we have explored several very different views in-so-far as its timing. One writer says it is about a war. Another says it is a celebration that takes place during the last year of the Tribulation when the redeemed are in heaven. Another says it will occur at the beginning of the Millennial Reign on earth after the Tribulation is over. Still another says it will occur in heaven as a glorious feast the Lord has prepared for His children. Other authors suggest that the Marriage Supper of the Lamb will not occur until sometime after the Millennial Reign of Christ [Messiah] when all of the redeemed are in heaven. Still others believe it will occur on the new earth after Satan and his cohorts have been destroyed. The timing of the Marriage Supper appears to be little understood. The timing suggested by this author attempts to explain away much of the confusion.

From Here – The Twenty-First Century to Eternity - To the Sabbath Rest

The eighth day is the beginning of the Sabbath Rest in heaven. It is the beginning of all things new. The redeemed of God can now rest because of their rescue from death and evil and their free gift of salvation purchased for them by Yeshua's sacrifice on the cross. The Jewish sages believed every day in heaven will be a Sabbath rest. For Christian believers, Yeshua Jesus is our Sabbath Rest!

Genesis 2:2-3 says, "By the seventh day God completed His work which He had done, and He rested on the seventh day from all His work which He had done. Then God blessed the seventh day and sanctified it, because in it He rested from all His work which God had created and made".

The Sabbath on earth is supposed to be a day to look forward to; a day to rest from one's labors, and focus on the blessings of God. It was meant to be a dress rehearsal of the days in heaven when every day is a day of Sabbath rest. Keeping the Sabbath was God's first commandment to man. It is written in Genesis 2. He later gave this commandment to Moses on Mount Sinai as part of the Hebrew "Ten Words", more commonly translated as the Ten Commandments.

I have spoken of the critical importance to man and God of the Sabbath rest, but as I look around our world today all I see is unrest.

The truth of Zechariah's warning about Jerusalem, in Zechariah 12:3, is happening: "It will come about in that day that I will make Jerusalem a heavy stone for all the peoples". Prophecy is being fulfilled before our eyes. Today the whole world is focused on Jerusalem and Israel. Anti-Semitism and anti-Christian sentiment continues to rise. Darkness and violence are filling the earth; from children murdering children, to gang members murdering those in authority, to violent games on social media, violent movies, and violence in the news media. Terror attacks are almost a daily occurrence. It is as if violence is being glorified to the point that people are becoming desensitized to it. Drug use, youth bullying other youth, suicide, and mental illness, and stress are on the increase.

There is estimated to be 43 wars of significance happening simultaneously at any one point in time. There are armed conflicts of nations against nations, ethnic groups against ethnic groups, political parties against political parties, acts of physical violence, and pressures all around the globe. With all of that turmoil, how does one find rest for their soul in modern life? The answer lies in faith in Yeshua Jesus, daily prayer, and trust in the knowledge that God is in charge and His Word is true. For far too many people, the world is so busy and noisy that they can't hear themselves think must less hear God's still, small voice. In many of the churches, social programs have been given priority over spiritual teaching and the study of the Scripture. It is as if the Lord is standing outside the door of His church knocking and asking to be invited in, but no one is listening. The world has overtaken the church rather than the church overtaking the world! It is proof we are living in the last of the last days! Everything in life is rush, rush, rush despite technological advances which are supposed to make life easier. In the workplace, technology is replacing many of the human workers so the few are taking over the work of the many, incomes are falling, inflation, lawlessness and crime are rising, and wars or rumors of war abound. All of this chaos was predicted in Matthew 24 to increase until the end of the Tribulation Period when Messiah will return to the earth at His second coming, and destroy all the evil that has been perpetrated on the earth by principalities and powers in high places, especially by those following Satan and other false gods. Matthew 24:22 warns of nuclear war when it says, "unless those days had been cut short, no life would have been saved; but for the sake of the elect those days will be cut short." God loves His children so much He has given us a warning. It is up to us to embrace it. Time is short. The time leading up to the Sabbath rest is close at hand. Still we humans resist and fail to see the handwriting on the wall. Because of our sin nature, we falsely believe we are in control, instead of God. But in the dark recesses of our mind we often wonder, why do I feel such unrest inside? We may try to shake it off by joking or by saying "there is no rest for the wicked", not realizing how true this statement is. It is no joking matter.

We fail to acknowledge that the lack of rest in this world is caused by having our priorities out of order. We put everything in our life ahead of God and by so doing fail to spend time in His presence. Our absence results in feelings of separation from Him, even though He is with us. To experience a sense of peace despite the turmoil around us, we need to restructure how we spend our days and make God a priority in our lives. If we don't put Him in first place we will be missing out on the greatest blessing of life, both in this world and the world to come. As we come to know God better, we will truly understand that He is a God of love who wants to richly bless His children. That is His heart's desire for us. He longs to spend time with His children. He wants us to know Him. We need to know who our God, Savior, and Messiah is, and what He did for us so long ago on that old, rugged cross. He is our rest. He alone is our peace. Putting this need on a human level, how can we deeply know who our children are, how they think, what they need, or what their goals are if we fail to spend the time to interact with them? The same is true of God. Scriptures tell us that God wants to spend time with His children and weeps when they ignore Him.

Isaiah 53 describes the Lord Yeshua for us; it says He was despised and forsaken of men; that he bore our sorrows, was pierced for our transgressions, crushed for our iniquities and by His scourging [stripes] we are healed. The book of Mark describes that Passover period and the events that occurred from Nisan 14 to Nisan 18. Imagine Yeshua Jesus on Nisan 14 as He struggled to carry His cross down the Via Dolorosa in Jerusalem after being tortured. He had been severely beaten [scourged] by the Roman soldiers that morning at the command of Pontius Pilate. Then had a crown made of thorns [likely made from either the thorn bush or Euphorbia milii] pressed into His forehead. He was weary as He carried the sins of the world on His back. It was just hours before that He had shared the Passover Seder with His disciples for the last time. A short time later Judas betrayed Him with a kiss to the chief priests, scribes, and elders. Yeshua had prayed in the Garden of Gethsemane for this cup to be removed from Him if it be His Father's will, while great drops of blood flowed from Him body from the emotional and physical stress of what He was about to experience. He was about to place the sins of the whole world onto Himself. All this He was willing to do for our redemption! Meanwhile His disciples kept falling asleep rather than praying with Him and offering comfort. He awoke them just as the accusers came to seize Him and took Him to the High Priest. Some men there broke one of the ten words by giving false testimonies. The High Priest accused Him of blasphemy and beat Him on His face during this sham of a trial, and Peter cursed and denied Him three times. He was taken before Pilate who offered Barabbas, a murderer as a substitute in his attempt to appease the crowd. He thought they would reject Barabbas whose Hebrew name was son (bar) of the father god (abba) but they accepted him instead of the true and only begotten Son of God, Yeshua, whose name means "salvation". He was hung and crucified on a wooden cross during Passover, buried in a borrowed tomb on the Feast of Unleavened Bread, and rose into heaven on the third day on the Feast of Firstfruits. He became the first fruit of all creation. He now sits on the right hand of the Father in heaven, with power. He is preparing a place for us, His bride, just as a bridegroom prepares a place for his bride here on earth.

A Trip to Golgotha and The Garden Tomb in Jerusalem

The grounds surrounding the Garden Tomb were beautiful. One immediately sensed a feeling of serenity. When we walked into the garden, the pathways were shaded by trees of various types and sizes, and flowers were blooming everywhere I looked. I remember going up a pathway toward a rock that is believed to be the place the Bible calls Golgotha, which means "the top of the hill". As I sat with other pilgrims on benches facing the rocky cliff, a large face of a skull was clearly visible. As we sat there our tour leader recounted the story of the cross and Yeshua's sacrifice on our behalf. Afterwards we walked down the shade-filled stony path which led to the tomb. The smell of the trees and flowers was sweet. After a short walk, we approached an opening where we could see a tomb carved in the side of a rock. It is believed by many to be the actual sepulchre in which Messiah was laid after His crucifixion. One by one we entered into the darkened tomb. A metal fence separated the viewing area from the two burial chambers that had been hollowed out inside the rock cave. The two chambers were each approximately six and a half feet long by four feet wide by 3 inches deep, and separated from one another by a small 2 inch high strip in the center. Each chamber could hold one corpse each. Outside the opening of the tomb was a carved out trench in which a large stone slab could have been rolled to cover the opening of the tomb. The right side of the tomb opening was enclosed by cinder blocks to protect the tomb from further deterioration. Close by the tomb was an old winepress. The stones on the pathway leading up to it have been estimated to be from the first century. This agrees with the biblical account of the location of the tomb of Yeshua our Messiah. Just outside the area of the tomb but facing it, were benches upon which we sat and had Communion. It was a deeply spiritual experience for all of us.

Yeshua Jesus, Our Bridegroom

Yeshua Jesus is the bridegroom to all who believe and put their faith in Him. Currently we are living in the period of time called the betrothal and are anxiously awaiting His return to take us home to be with Him throughout eternity. He said, "in my Father's house are many mansions, if it were not so I would have told you; for I go to prepare a place for you. If I go and prepare a place for you, I will come again and receive you to Myself, that where I am, there you may be also"– John 14:2-3. While we wait, we have been called to live our lives set apart as one who is betrothed to the King of kings. We are to commune with Him and have no other god's except Him. Since the Feast of Pentecost in the first century, the Christian church has been preparing for the Lord's return. While we wait, He gave us a bridal gift to show His love for us. He sent the gift of the Holy Spirit which has sealed us as a sign of our betrothal to Messiah. The final events will begin with the Rapture of the church when all believers who have put their trust in Him will hear Him call, "come up here" from the clouds and will forever be with the Lord. His bride will be given their glorified bodies that can not be destroyed. We will again return to earth with Him at the end of the Tribulation Period.

Here He will destroy all the armies of His enemies in the last battle of Armageddon. Afterwards, the bride will live on the new heaven and on the new earth – Revelation 21:1-6. The earth will be transformed like it was in the beginning in the Garden of Eden. All things will be made new. Yeshua will reign and rule with a fist of iron, and the tabernacle of God will now be dwelling with men. Children born during the 1,000 year reign of Yeshua will be given the opportunity to accept Yeshua as their Messiah, and become part of God's plan on earth or reject Him and be damned for eternity. The choice will be made based on the fact they have lived in a perfect environment that will be glorious, and under the reign of Yeshua where justice and fairness is the rule. The New Jerusalem will have come down from heaven and dwell on the earth. This city replaces the old and the Temple will once more be filled with the Shekinah glory of the Lord. Then Satan will be loosed on the earth for an unknown period of time again. Once more mankind will be given the choice of heaven or hell. After this period, Satan and his followers will be thrown into the Lake of fire where they will remain for eternity.

The restoration of the earth and the transformation of the bride will now be complete. Eternity awaits God's children, an eternity in which to explore the depths of His love, beauty, and grace. While in heaven all of the redeemed will participate in the Marriage Supper of the Lamb. The bride will be made into the image of her Messiah, without spot or blemish, and she will be freed from the curse of sin.

The Jews Resettle in the Promised Land

God promised future grace on the land and people of Israel in Jeremiah 33:10-11. It says, "Thus says the Lord, 'Yet again there will be heard in this place of which you say, "It is a waste, without man and without beast," that is, in the cities of Judah and in the streets of Jerusalem that are desolate, without man and without inhabitant and without beast, the voice of joy and the voice of gladness, the voice of the bridegroom and the voice of the bride, the voice of those who say, "Give thanks to the Lord of hosts, For the Lord is good, For His loving kindness is everlasting"; and of those who bring a thank offering into the house of the Lord, For I will restore the fortunes of the land as they were at first, says the Lord."

The writer Mark Twain visited the Holy Land in 1867. He described it as "a desolate country" and "a land devoid of both vegetation and human population". He said the soil was covered over with weeds and that the city of Jerusalem was so small that one could walk around it in an hour. The population was about 25,000. Today we are seeing God's grace toward His chosen people and His city being filled. On May 14, 1948 Israel became a nation again after 2,000 years. When they arrived it was indeed waste land, without the presence of man or beast, still the Jews paid the Arabs for what appeared to be worthless soil and invited them to work as coworkers together in the land. [An invitation many now believe was a mistake.] Many Jews experienced malaria as they cleared the swamps, others had to learn how to farm the land and plant the crops, and still others built the cities or joined the military. The Jews all worked together to turn the desert into a garden of fruit and flowers. After the Six Day War in 1967 they regained control of Jerusalem, their capital and eternal city. Now their population has reached almost 866,000 and they are proud of their land God has returned to them. While many are not yet believers in Yeshua Jesus, many of the young are coming to the saving grace of Yeshua, their Messiah and are looking forward to a glorious hereafter.

The glorious hereafter will center on the person of Yeshua Mashiach, the anointed one, the Messiah. It is written in the Talmud, that all rabbis' agree that Mashiach will be a divinely appointed human being who will carry out a specific task. They believe He will be a descendant of King David and will be called "the son of David". He will be a man acquainted with grief and sorrow – Isaiah 53. He will arrive to this world at a time when the earth will be in a state of utter demoralization and when political unrest ushers in a bitter war. The rabbis' further believe that the Messiah will return to renew the world after 7,000 years [after Adam and Eve were created by God], that Israel's oppression by a hostile world will end, and Israel will be restored to a position of eminence. The re-gathering of the tribes of Israel from the lands where they have been scattered is happening. Many people believe the third Temple will be rebuilt soon. They celebrate the fact that President Donald Trump of America will transfer the American embassy from Tel Aviv to Jerusalem and participate in the 70th year celebration of their return to the land God promised them. Other nations are following his lead and move their embassy to Jerusalem in recognition that it is the eternal city of the Jews and of God.

The Jewish people see this life as preliminary to another higher life. They acknowledge the fact that God gave them three special gifts: "the Torah, the land of Israel, and the World to Come". "In the world to come, there will be no eating or drinking; no procreation of children or business transaction; no envy or hatred or rivalry; but the righteous sit enthroned, their crown on their head, and enjoy the luster of the Shechinah".

Eight Things the Messiah will do in the hereafter:

1. He will illumine the world with His light. No other light is needed- Revelation 23: 23-24
2. The trees will produce twelve kinds of fruit every month and all persons who eat of their fruit will be healed – Revelation 22:2.
3. Yeshua Jesus will build the holy Temple in Jerusalem with precious stones and He will rule and reign from there - Zechariah 6:11-16 and Revelation 21:14.
4. "The redeemed are the stones that make up the holy city" – Pastor Biltz.
5. Peace will reign in nature – the wolf will dwell with the lamb - Isaiah 11:6.
6. He will dry the tears from everyone's eyes- Revelation 21:4
7. There will be no more death – Revelation 21:4.
8. Everyone will be happy and have joy inexpressible and full of glory - I Peter 1:8.

When will Messiah Come To Rescue the Jewish people?

Jewish sages through the years have written many ideas concerning the timing of when the Messiah, the son of David, will come to save the Jewish people. Some have said the Messiah won't come until there is a generation on the earth that is altogether righteous. Another has penned that He will come at a time when there is a great war on the earth. A third Sage has said that the Messiah won't come until the treasure of souls is empty. The Old Testament gives a truer picture of the Lord's coming. Isaiah 59:19-20 says "So they will fear the name of the Lord from the west and His glory from the rising of the sun, for He will come like a rushing stream which the wind of the Lord drives, a Redeemer will come to Zion, and to those who turn from transgression in Jacob, declares the Lord"." [have been used up], Isaiah 57:16. Zechariah 9:9 says, "Rejoice greatly, O daughter of Zion, shout in triumph, O daughter of Jerusalem! behold, your king is coming to you, he is just and endowed with salvation, humble, and mounted on a donkey; even on a colt, the foal of a donkey".

To know the timing, as Christians, we believe the words of Yeshua Jesus who said He would not come back until the Jewish people call out for Him whom they had pierced, and they will mourn for Him, as one mourns for an only son, and they will weep bitterly over Him like the bitter weeping over a firstborn – Zechariah 12:10. We also must remember that it was when Judah repented the Joseph, a type of Yeshua, revealed himself – Genesis 45:3. It appears then that the Jews will call out to Yeshua at the end of the Tribulation Period. In Matthew 23:37-39 Yeshua is lamenting over Jerusalem. He says, "Jerusalem, Jerusalem, who kills the prophets and stones those who are sent to her! How often I wanted to gather your children together, the way a hen gathers her chicks under her wings, and you were unwilling. Behold, your house is being left to you desolate! For I say to you, from now on you will not see Me until you say, 'Blessed is He who comes in the name of the Lord!'"

Song:

The outstretched arms of Messiah
As He sits on His heavenly throne,
Are reaching out to His children,
To join Him in His eternal home.

Appendix 1

Pictures taken by Mr. Reuven Prager of the bride's crown, aperion, and chuppah chatanim are presented here. Mr. Prager discovered these items while doing research on the ancient Jewish wedding. Each item was made as authentic as possible. A picture of the groom's crown of roses and myrtle, however, is not available at this time.

End Notes

CHAPTER 1: The Sabbath

1 Leviticus 23:1-3
2 Genesis 2:3
3 Michael, Boaz. The Fruits of Zion Magazine
4 Genesis 1:2-4
5 Isaiah 58:13-14
6 Genesis 48:20
7 Psalm 31
8 Psalm 1
9 Genesis 48:20
10 Ruth 4:11
11 Numbers 6:24-26
12 Psalm 104:15
13 Psalm 24:3-4
14 Numbers 18:19
15 Deuteronomy 8:10
16 Psalm 48:1
17 Exodus 20:8
18 Genesis 2:3
19 Isaiah 11:1-5
20 Encyclopedia Britannica – The Counsel of Nicea
21 Hadler, Sam. Messiah in the Feasts of Israel, Word of Messiah Ministries, 2006, 2010
22 Revelation 19:16
23 Exodus 20:8
24 Mark 11:9

CHAPTER 2: Overview of the Feasts

1 Leviticus 23:2-4
2 Bernis, Jonathan - quote
3 Exodus 12:3-10,13,14
4 I Samuel 15:22
5 Isaiah 1:11-17
6 John 19:17
7 Numbers 21:9
8 Genesis 48:14
9 Exodus 12
10 John 19:31-34
11 Exodus 13:6-7
12 II Corinthians 5:21
13 Leviticus 23:10-12
14 Norton, Michael. Unlocking the Secrets of the Feasts: The Prophecies in the Feasts of Leviticus, Westbow Press, 2012, 2015
15 Exodus 19
16 Leviticus 23:24-25
17 Revelation 11:15
18 Revelation 23:24
19 I Corinthians 15:51-53
20 Leviticus 23:27
21 Leviticus 23:42-43
22 Mark 11:8-9
23 John 10:22-23
24 Esther 9:22

CHAPTER THREE: The Feast of Purim

1 Isaiah 45:1-7
2 Esther 9:26
3 Biltz, Mark, Pastor – Archive Lecture on Purim, 2017
4 Ibid
5 Ibid
6 Genesis 36:12
7 Isaiah 14:13-14
8 Ezekiel 28:19
9 Deuteronomy 31:16
10 Daniel 1:7

11 John 1:7-9
12 II Corinthians 9:15
13 Numbers 13:25-33
14 Genesis 23:7
15 Exodus 17:23-19
16 Proverbs 23:19-35

CHAPTER FOUR: The Feast of Passover

1 Michael Norton. Unlocking the Secrets of the Feasts: The Prophecies in the Book of Leviticus, Westbow Press, 2012, 2015
2 Chuck Missler, Dr., The Feasts of Israel. Koinonia House, Inc., Coeur d'Alene, ID. 2016
3 Exodus 1:8
4 Mark Biltz, Pastor. Archives on Passover, 2015, 2017.
5 Exodus 1:10
6 Exodus 2:2-3
7 Exodus 2:10
8 Exodus 4:21
9 Exodus 5:2
10 Biltz, Mark, Pastor. Archives on Passover, 2015, 2017
11 Exodus 11:4-5, 7
12 Psalm 51:16-17, 19
13 Exodus 12:13
14 Rosen, Ceil and Moishe. Christ in the Passover: Why is This Night Different?
15 Moody Press, Chicago, IL., 1978.
16 Luke 19:46
17 Numbers 9:1-13
18 Stone, Perry. CD #112, Disc 6: The Shini.
19 Josephus: Complete Works. Public Domain. Kregel Publications, Grand Rapids, MI.
20 Stone, Perry. CD: The Shini
21 Psalm 113-118
22 Exodus 12:14
23 Luke 22:17
24 Luke 22:21
25 Luke 22:20
26 Luke 22:18
27 Rosen, Ceil and Moishe. Christ in the Passover: Why is This Night Different? Moody Press, Chicago, IL., 1978.
28 John 13:21-27

29 I Corinthians 11:23-24
30 Matthew 26:36
31 Matthew 27:5
32 Stone, Perry. Television program: MannaFest. Teaching.
33 Matthew 27:9
34 Cahn, Jonathan, Rabbi. The Book of Mysteries. FrontLine, Charisma Media/ Charisma House Book Group, Lake Mary, FL., 2016. Page 43, titled: The Asham.
35 Andrews, William MD. On the Physical Death of Jesus Christ, The Journal of the American Medical Association article, Vol. 256, 1986.
36 Josephus: Complete Works. Public Domain. Kregel Publications, Grand Rapids, MI.
37 Missler, Chuck, Dr. The Feast of Israel. Koinonia House, Inc., Coeur d'Alene, ID. 2016.
38 John 19:22
39 Biltz, Mark, Pastor. Archived teaching on Passover, 2015, 2016, 2017
40 Rubin, Barry and Steffi. The Messianic Passover Haggadah, Revised and Updated. Messianic Jewish Publishers, Clarksville, MD, 1989, 2005.
41 Biltz, Mark, Pastor. The Passover Seder for Believers in Yeshua. El Shaddai Ministries, 2016.
42 Biltz, Mark, Pastor. Archived teachings on Passover, 2015, 2017
43 Ibid
44 Leviticus 1:1-17, 6:8-13
45 Leviticus 2:1-16, 6:14-23
46 Leviticus 3:1-17, 7:11-36
47 Leviticus 4: 1-5, 6:24-27
48 Leviticus 5:14, 6:7, 7:1-7
49 Cahn, Jonathan, Rabbi. The Book of Mysteries. FrontLine, Charisma Media/ Charisma House Book Group, Lake Mary, FL., 2016, p.77 titled: The Priests of the Offering.
50 Klein, Ken. Petra: Israel's Secret Hiding Place, DVD. kenkleinproductions.net
51 Genesis 27
52 II Samuel 8

CHAPTER FIVE: The Feast of Unleavened Bread

1 Rosen, Ceil and Moishe. Christ of the Passover: Why is This Night Different? Moody Press, Chicago, IL. 1978.
2 Leviticus 23:6
3 Booker, Richard, Dr. Celebrating Jesus in the Biblical Feasts, Expanded Edition. Destiny Image Publishers, Inc, Shippensburg, PA., 2016.

4 Norton, Michael. Unlocking the Secrets of the Feasts: The Prophecies in the Feast of Leviticus. Westbow Press, Nashville, TN., 2012.
5 Ibid – Booker
6 Missler, Chuck, Dr. The Feasts of Israel. Koinonia House, Coeur d'Alene, ID, 2016.
7 Ibid- Booker, Richard, Dr.
8 Matthew 28:6
9 Matthew 28:3-4

CHAPTER SIX: The Feast of Firstfruits

1 Baker, Todd Dr. The Feast of Firstfruits. The Levitt Letter., Box 12268, Dallas, TX. 2017.
2 Deuteronomy 8:8
3 Leviticus 23:9-11
4 Norton, Michael. Unlocking the Secrets of the Feasts: The Prophecies in the Feasts of Leviticus. Westbow Press, Nashville, TN., 2012, 2015.
5 Nadler, Sam. Messiah in the Feasts of Israel, Revised Edition. Word of Messiah Ministries, 2006, 2010.
6 Revelation 14:1

CHAPTER SEVEN: The Feast of Shavuot/Pentecost

1 Stearman, Gary. "Pentecost 2017: Reviewing the Rapture. Prophecy Watcher, 06/2017, pp. 4–7, 10, 20-21.
2 Missler, Chuck, Dr. The Feasts of Israel. Koinonia House, Coeur d'Alene, ID., 2016.
3 Exodus 19:16-20
4 Exodus 19:13
5 Psalm 29:3-9
6 Norton, Michael. Unlocking the Secrets of the Feasts; The Prophecies in the Feasts of Leviticus. WestBow Press, Nashville, TN., 2012, 2015
7 Acts 2:2-6
8 Booker, Richard Dr. Celebrating Jesus in the Biblical Feasts, Expanded Edition. Destiny Image Publishers, Inc., Shippensburg, PA., 2016
9 Joel 2: 28-29
10 Genesis 8:7
11 II Peter 5:8
12 Ruth 2:8-10
13 Ruth 4:1
14 Ibid – Stearman, Gary.

CHAPTER EIGHT: The Feast of Trumpets/Rosh Hashanah

1 Leviticus 23:23-25
2 Genesis 22:13
3 I Thessalonians 4:16-17
4 I Thessalonians 5:2
5 Isaiah 64:6
6 Psalm 47:1-2, 5-8
7 Jeremiah 30:7
8 Genesis 22:13
9 Numbers 10:2-3
10 Biltz, Mark Pastor. God's Day Timer. WND Books, Washington, DC, 2016.
11 Evans, Michael, Dr. Rosh Hashanah. Friends of Zion. Magazine of the Jerusalem Prayer Team International, September, 2016.
12 Isaiah 62:6
13 Ezekiel 33:3-4
14 Joel 2: 1-2

CHAPTER NINE: Yom Kippur/Day of Atonement

1 Biltz, Mark, Pastor. Archives on Yom Kippur, 2016 and on handout
2 Revelation 19:2, 13-15
3 Deuteronomy 9:17-18
4 Exodus 32:32
5 Leviticus 23:26-31
6 Jonah 1:3
7 Jonah 2:10
8 Ibid - Biltz, Mark, Pastor.
9 Nadler, Sam. Messiah in the Feasts of Israel, Revised Edition. Word of Messiah Ministries, 2006, 2010.
10 I John 1:9
11 Leviticus 16:3-5
12 Leviticus 16:10
13 Ibid – Nadler, Sam.
14 Leviticus 17:14
15 Hebrews 10:6

CHAPTER TEN: The Feast of Sukkot/Tabernacles

1 Deuteronomy 16:16
2 Revelation 7:9
3 Zechariah 14:16-17
4 Leviticus 23:39-43
5 Psalm 139:7-12
6 Biltz, Mark, Pastor. Archives Feast of Sukkot, 2016, teaching on Sabbath.
7 Ibid, Cahn, Jonathan Rabbi.
8 Norton, Michael. Unlocking the Secrets of the Feasts: The Prophecies in the Feasts of Leviticus. WestBow Press, Nashville, TN, 2012, 2015.
9 Nadler, Sam. Messiah in the Feasts of Israel, Revised Edition. Word of Messiah Ministries, 2006, 2010.
10 Stone, Perry, Jr. Breaking the Code of the Feasts: Discover Future Prophetic Events in the Feasts and Special Celebrations of Israel! Voice of Evangelism Outreach Ministries, Inc., Cleveland, TN. 2007
11 Psalm 118:25
12 Ibid – Biltz, Mark Pastor
13 Isaiah 12:3
14 John 7:37-39
15 John 8
16 Numbers 29:35-36
17 Deuteronomy 34
18 Zechariah 12:10
19 John 12:12-13
20 Revelation 7:9
21 Micah 5:2
22 Luke 2:1-3
23 Luke 2:8
24 Micah 4:8
25 Genesis 35:19-24
26 Micah 5:2
27 Luke 13:15
28 Joel 2:28
29 Hosea 3:5
30 Biltz, Mark Pastor. Sabbath teaching on the Six Things About Yeshua in the Scriptures, 2017.

CHAPTER 11: The Feast of Chanukah

1 Daniel 8:3-11
2 Goldwurm, Hersh Rabbi, Meir Zlotowitz, Rabbi, and Nosson Scherman, Rabbi. Chanukah: Its History, Observance, and Significance. ArtScroll Mesorah Series by Mesorah Publications, ltd., New York, 1981, 2005
3 Daniel 11:31-33
4 Ibid – Goldwurm, Hersh Rabbi.
5 John 10:22-24
6 John 10:31
7 Daniel 9:26
8 Revelation 17:14
9 Revelation 19:20-21
10 John 6:6-9, 9:5
11 Matthew 24
12 I Thessalonians 5:25

CHAPTER 12: The Ancient Jewish Wedding and The Feast of the Lord

1 Genesis 2:18, 21, 24
2 Genesis 1:28
3 Cahn, Jonathan Rabbi. CD, The Mystery of the Bride and the Groom.
4 Matthew 1:20
5 Psalm 61:10, 62:5
6 Prager, Reuvin. Reviving Biblical Wedding Customs in Preparation for the Third Temple. Breaking Israel News: Latest News Biblical Perspective, March 20, 2018, 2:00 pm and personal email conversations.
7 Psalm 45
8 Isaiah 61:10-62:5
9 Psalm 137:5

CHAPTER 13: The Marriage Supper of the Lamb

1 Matthew 22:2-4
2 Luke 14:16-24
3 I Thessalonians 4:16-18
4 I Corinthians 15:51-53
5 II Corinthians 5:10
6 Zechariah 14:5
7 Revelation 6:10

8 Psalm 50:5
9 Matthew 24:31
10 Joel 2:11
11 Revelation 19:9, 14-15
12 Revelation 15:4
13 Isaiah 13:3
14 Davis, Susan, Dictated. Marriage Supper of the Lamb: And End Time Events: Words For This Last Generation. end-times-prophecy.com, 2012, p. 31-34.
15 I Corinthians 2:9
16 John 14:1-3
17 Revelation 19:7, 9
18 Revelation 20:10

CHAPTER 14: The Sabbath Rest

1 Genesis 2:2-3
2 Zechariah 12:3
3 Matthew 24:1-22
4 Isaiah 53
5 John 14:2-3
6 Revelation 21:1-6
7 Jeremiah 33:10-11
8 Isaiah 53
9 Revelation 21:23-24
10 Zechariah 6:11-16
11 Revelation 21:14
12 Revelation 21:4
13 Isaiah 59:19-20
14 Isaiah 57:16
15 Zechariah 12:10
16 Matthew 23:37-39
17 Genesis 45:3
18 I Peter 1:8

Bibliography

Baker, Todd, Dr. Feast of Firstfruits. The Levitt Letter. Box 12268, Dallas, TX.

Bernis, Jonathan. *The Feast of Israel: A Revelation of Messiah and the Last Days Prophecy*. Jewish Voice Ministries International, 2 CD's, www.jewishvoice.org.

Biltz, Mark. *The Feasts of the Lord: Passover to Pentecost, Yom Teruah, Feast of Tabernacles, Yom Kippur, Study Guide and Notes*. El Shaddai Ministries, 2008.

2. Sabbath lessons taught over a period of five years in the archives
3. Booklet: The Passover Seder: For Believers in Yeshua. El Shaddai Ministries, 2016.
4. God's Day Timer, WND Books Publisher, 2016

Booker, Richard Dr. *Celebrating Jesus in the Biblical Feasts*, Expanded Edition. Destiny

Image Publishers, Inc., 2016.

Cahn, Rabbi Jonathan. Hope of the World.org

1. The Book of Mysteries, p. 43 and 77
2. *The Mystery of the Bride and Bridegroom*, CD #1425, 2011.
3. *The Birthdate of Yeshua*, YouTube and the Jim Bakker Show
4. The Mystery of the Shabbath Codes
5. The Mystery of Haman 1 CD #1801, 2013

Davis, Susan. *Marriage Supper of the Lamb: From the Heart of God*. end-times prophecy.com, 2012.

Evans, Dr. Michael. *Rosh Hashanah*. Magazine of the Jerusalem Prayer Team International, September, 2016.

Franz, Gordon. *Jesus Celebrated Purim.* Lambert Dolphin's Library, 03/05/03.

Goldwurn, Hersh Rabbi, Zlotowitz, Meir Rabbi, Scherman, Nosson Rabbi. *Chanukah: Its History, Observance, and Significance/A presentation Based Upon Talmudic and Traditional Sources.* Mesorah Publications, ltd, Brooklyn, New York 2005.

Klein, Ken. *Petra: Israel's Secret Hiding Place.* DVD, Kenklein productions.net

Michael, Boaz. *Which Day Is the Sabbath Day?* Fruits of Zion, Messiah Magazine, Volume 2, Issue 12, Winter, 2017.

Missler, Chuck, Dr., *The Feasts of Israel.* Koinonia House, Inc., Coeur d'Alene, ID., 2016.

2. Missler, Chuck, Dr., *The 7th Day, 2017.* Koinonia House, Inc., Coeur D'Alene, ID.

Nadler, Sam. *Messiah in the Feasts of Israel:* Revised Edition. Word of Messiah

Ministries, Charlotte, N.C., 2010.

New American Standard Bible, Wide Margin, Zondervan, Grand Rapids, Michigan, 1995.

Norten, Michael. *Unlocking the Secrets of the Feasts: The Prophecies in the Feast of Leviticus.* Westbow Press, 2012.

Prager, Reuven. *Reviving Biblical Wedding Customs in Preparation for the Third Temple.* Breaking Israel News, March 20, 2018.

Rubin, Barry. *The Messianic Passover Haggadah.* Messianic Jewish Publishers,

Clarksville, Maryland, 1998.

Rosen, Ceil and Moishe. *Christ in the Passover: Why is This Night Different?* Moody

Press, Chicago, IL., 1978.

Stapleton, Tom. Fulfillment of Sanctuary Types: Spring Feasts, YouTube, 03/13/2017.

Stearman, Gary. *Pentecost 2017: Reviewing the Rapture.* Prophecy Watcher, 06/2017.

Stone, Jr., Perry. *Breaking the Code of the Feasts: Discover Future Prophetic Events in the Feasts and Special Celebrations of Israel.* Voice of Evangelism, Cleveland, TN, 2007.

2. *The Passover Shini*, CD #112, Disc 6.

The Editors of Encyclopaedia Britannica. *Council of Nicaea.* Encyclopaedia Britannica, 01/28/2009.

The Journal of the American Medical Association. *On the Physical Death of Jesus Christ.* March 21, 1986, Volume 256.

The Complete Jewish Study Bible: Insights for Jews and Christians: Illuminating the Jewishness of God's Word. Messianic Jewish Publishers and Resources. Hendrickson Bibles.

The Hours Before Jesus' Crucifixion, Bible Studies Fellowship International, 2016.

Whiston, William A.M., Translator. *Josephus: Complete Works.* Kregel Publications, Grand Rapids, Michigan, 1981.

Printed in the United States
By Bookmasters